Cute Fox
Coloring Book For
Adults

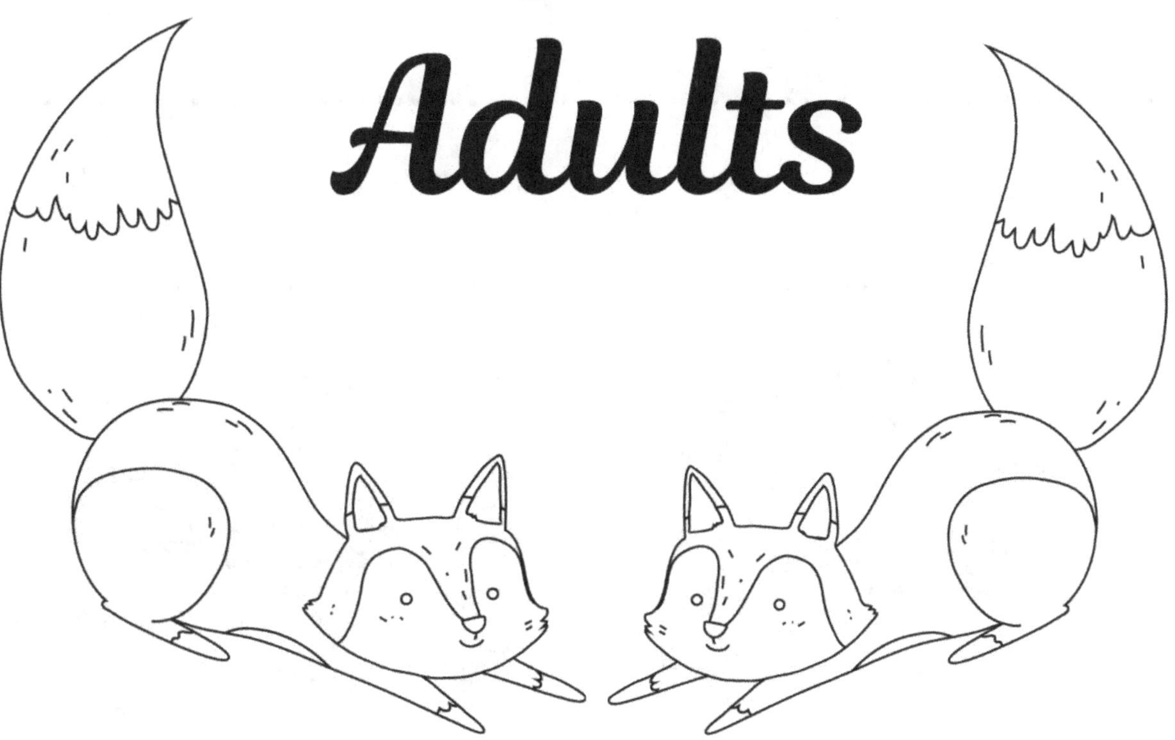

This Book Belongs

To...

· ·

· ·

· ·

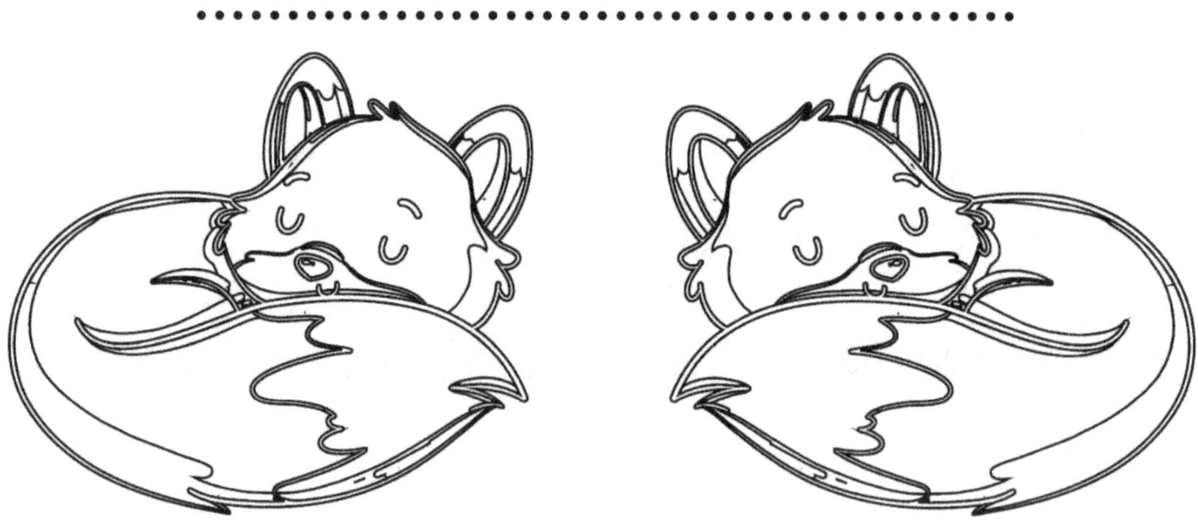

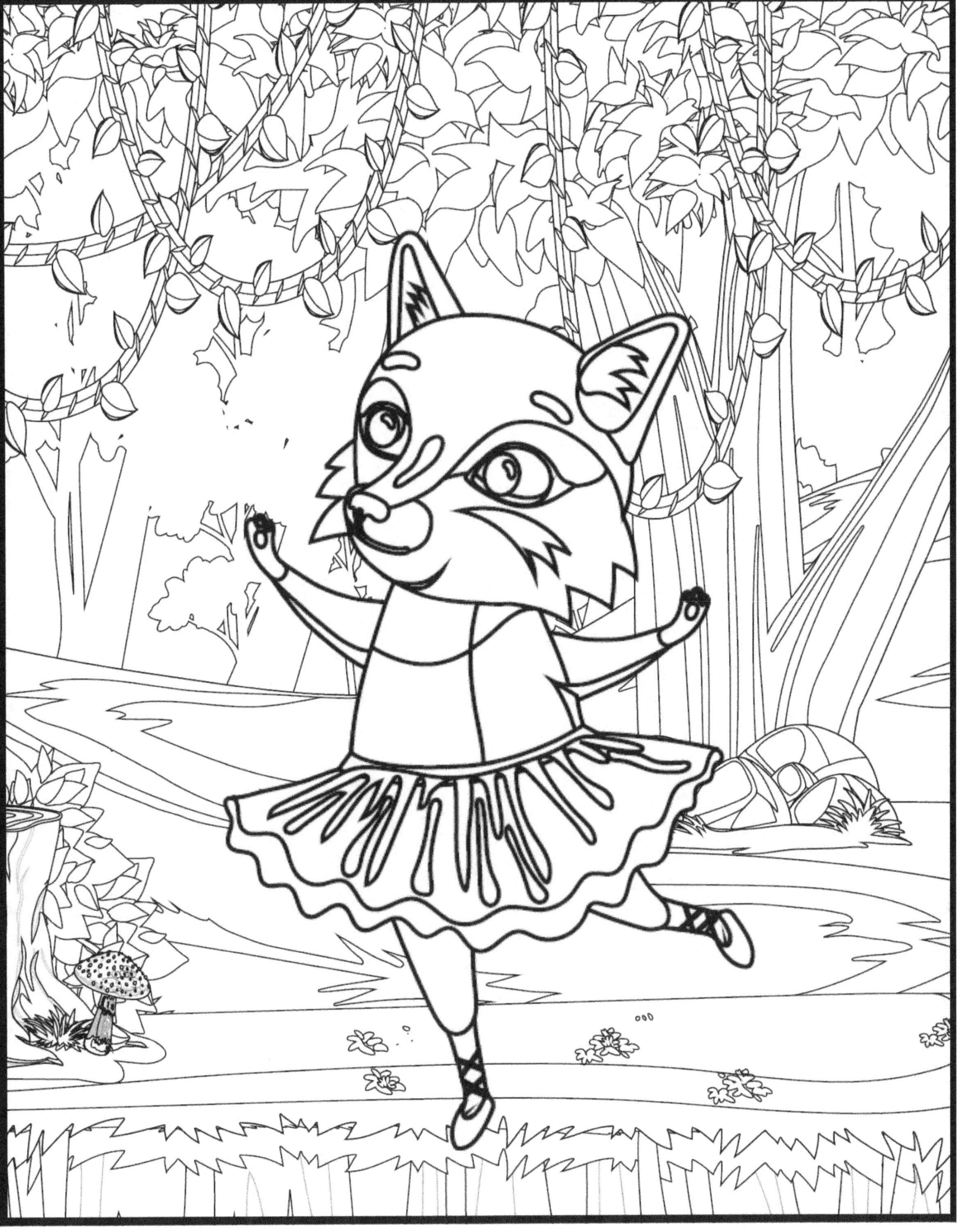

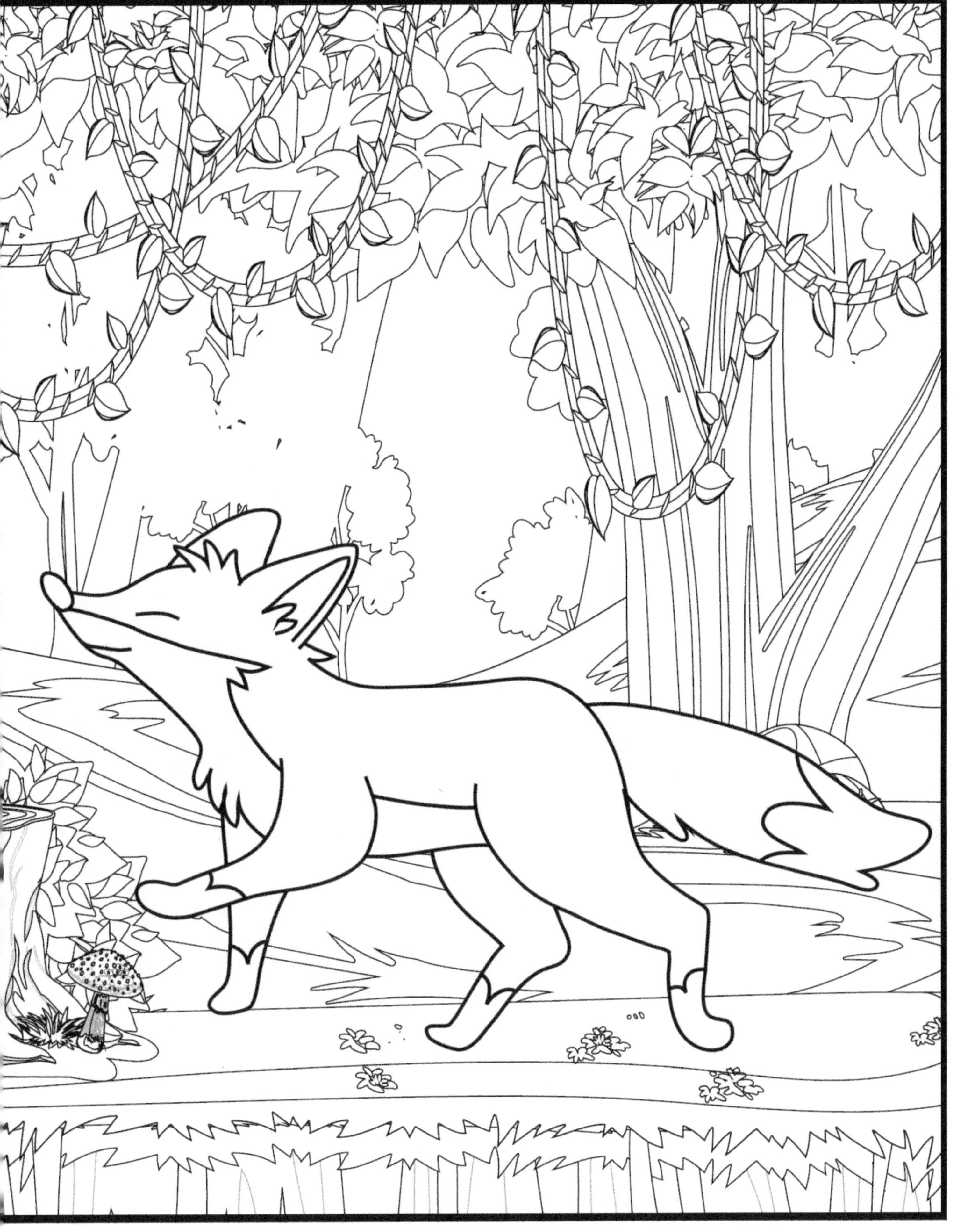

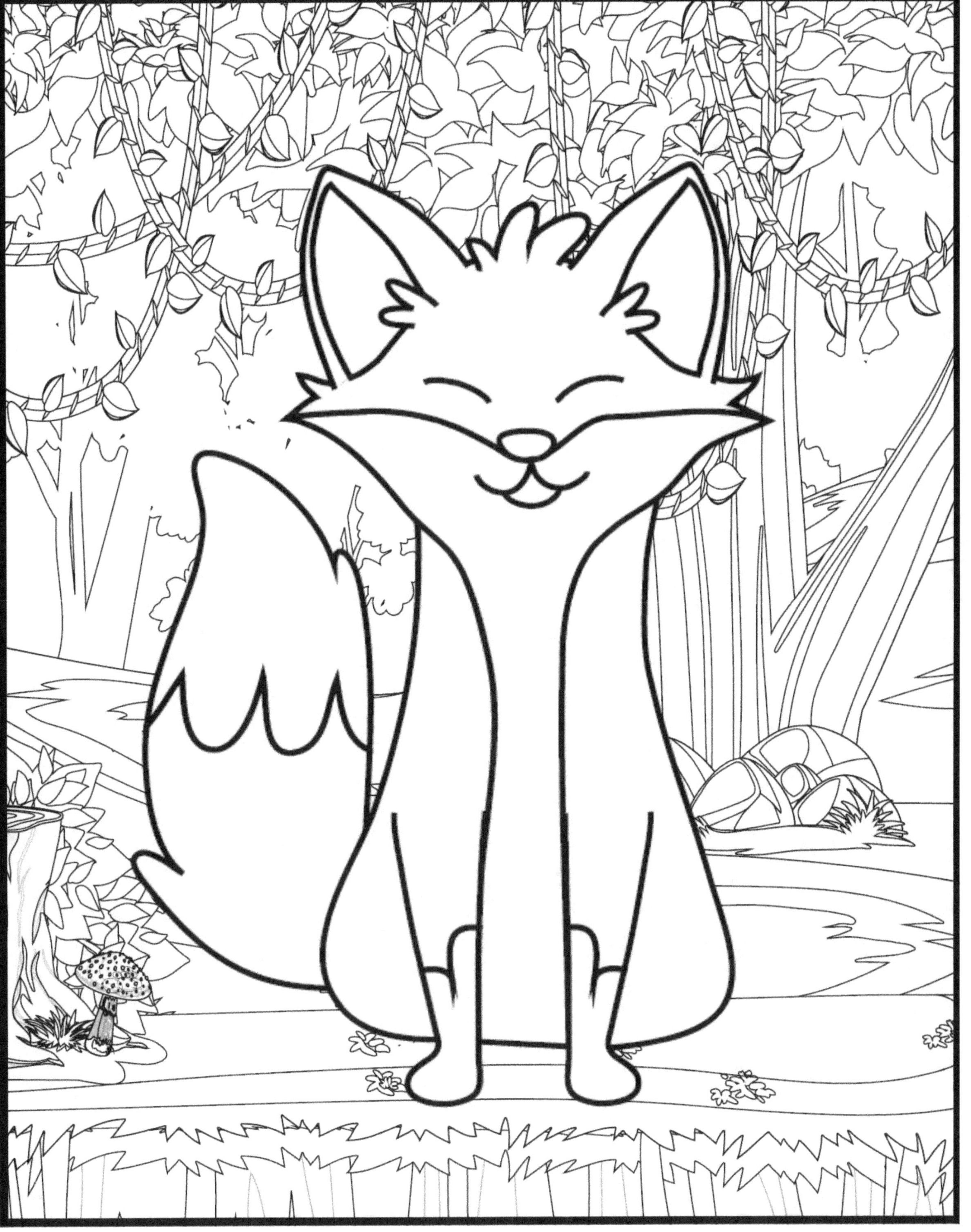

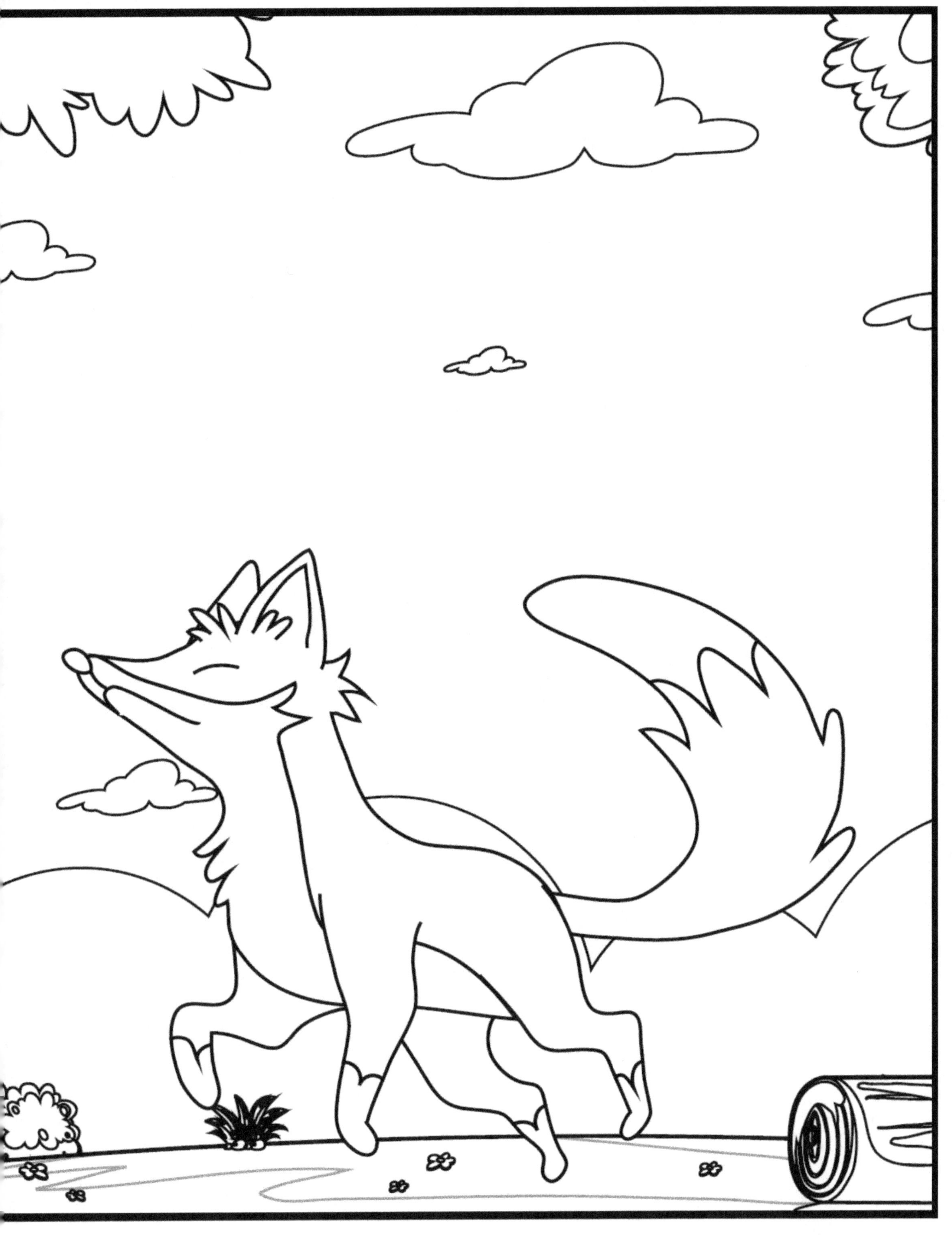

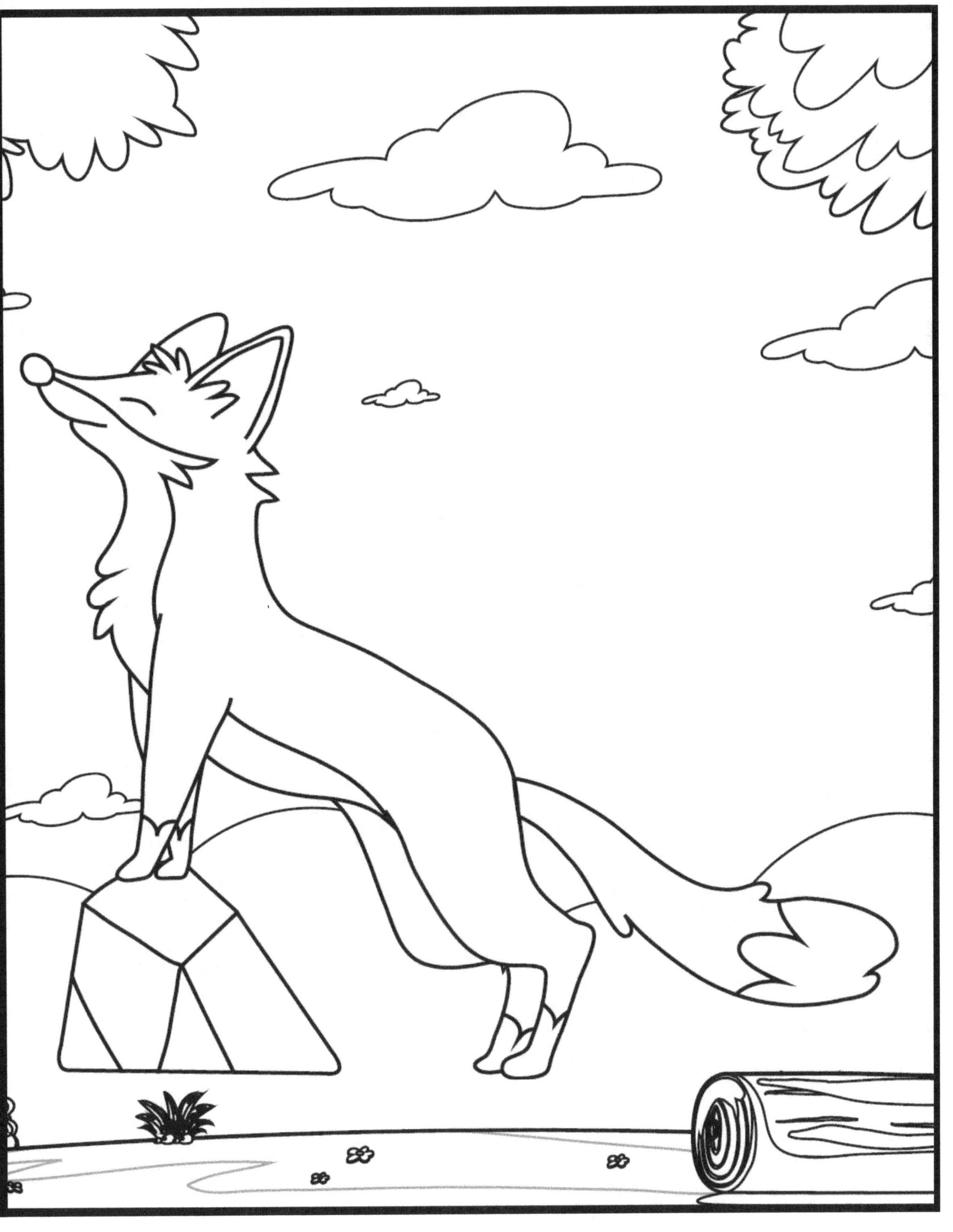

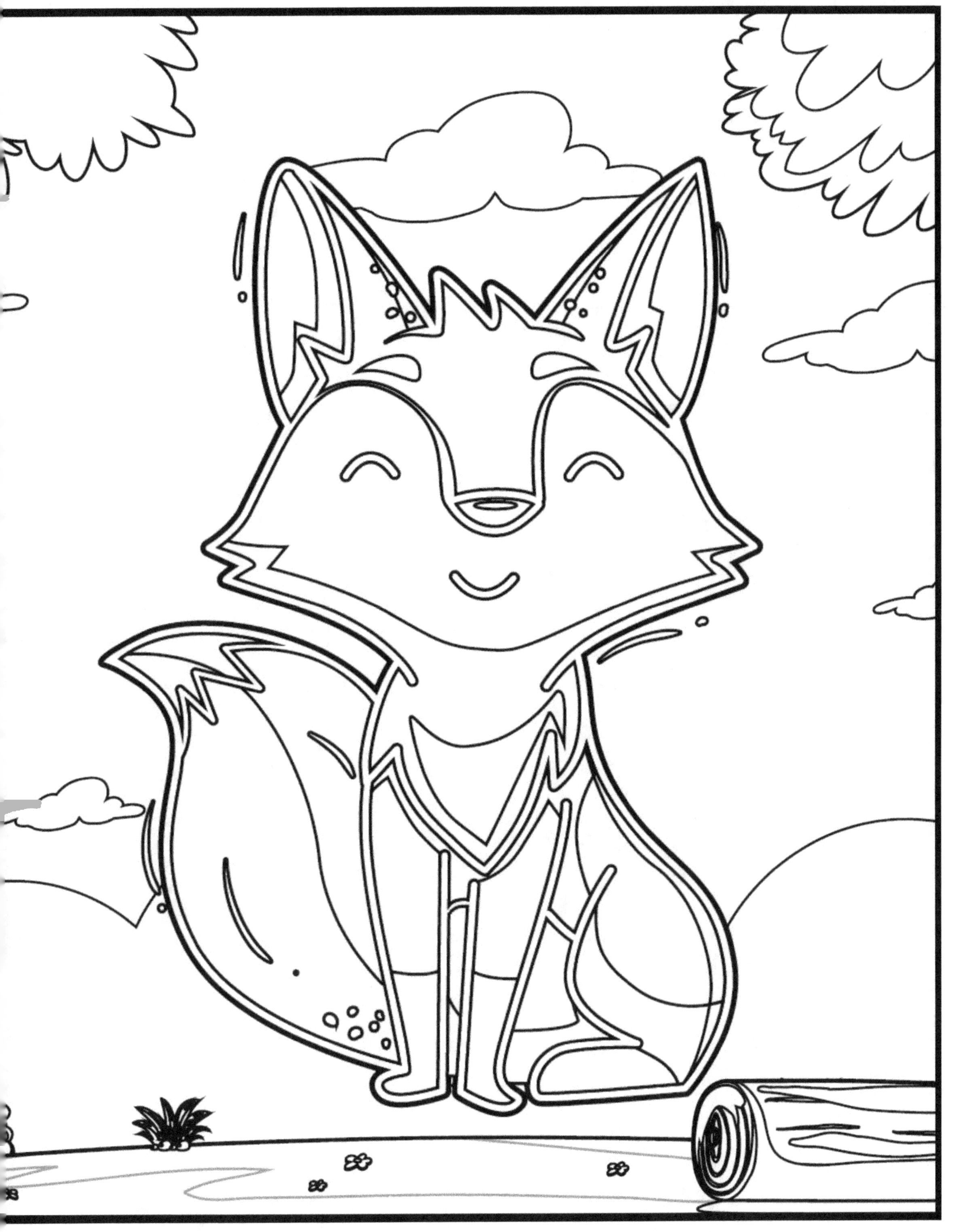

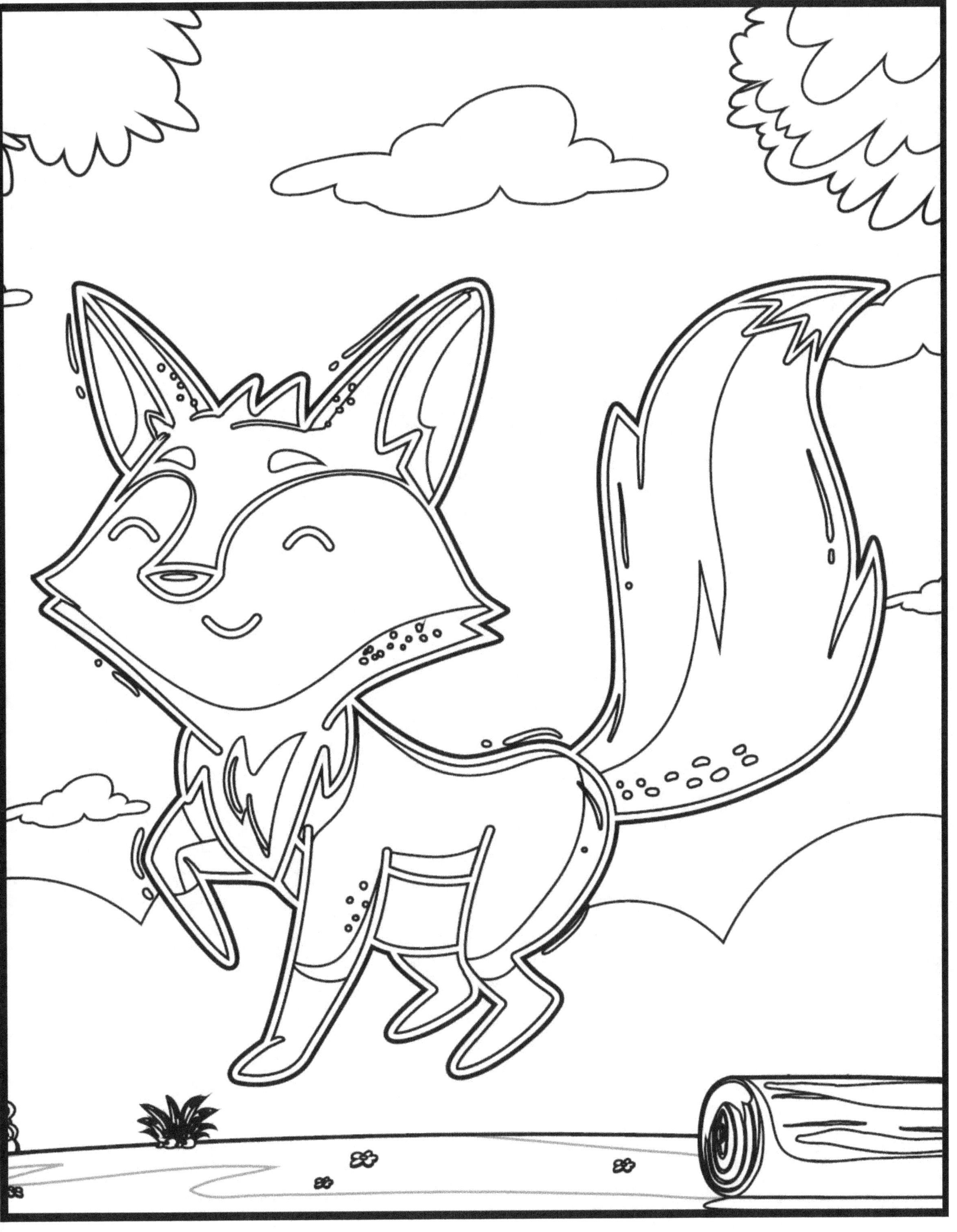

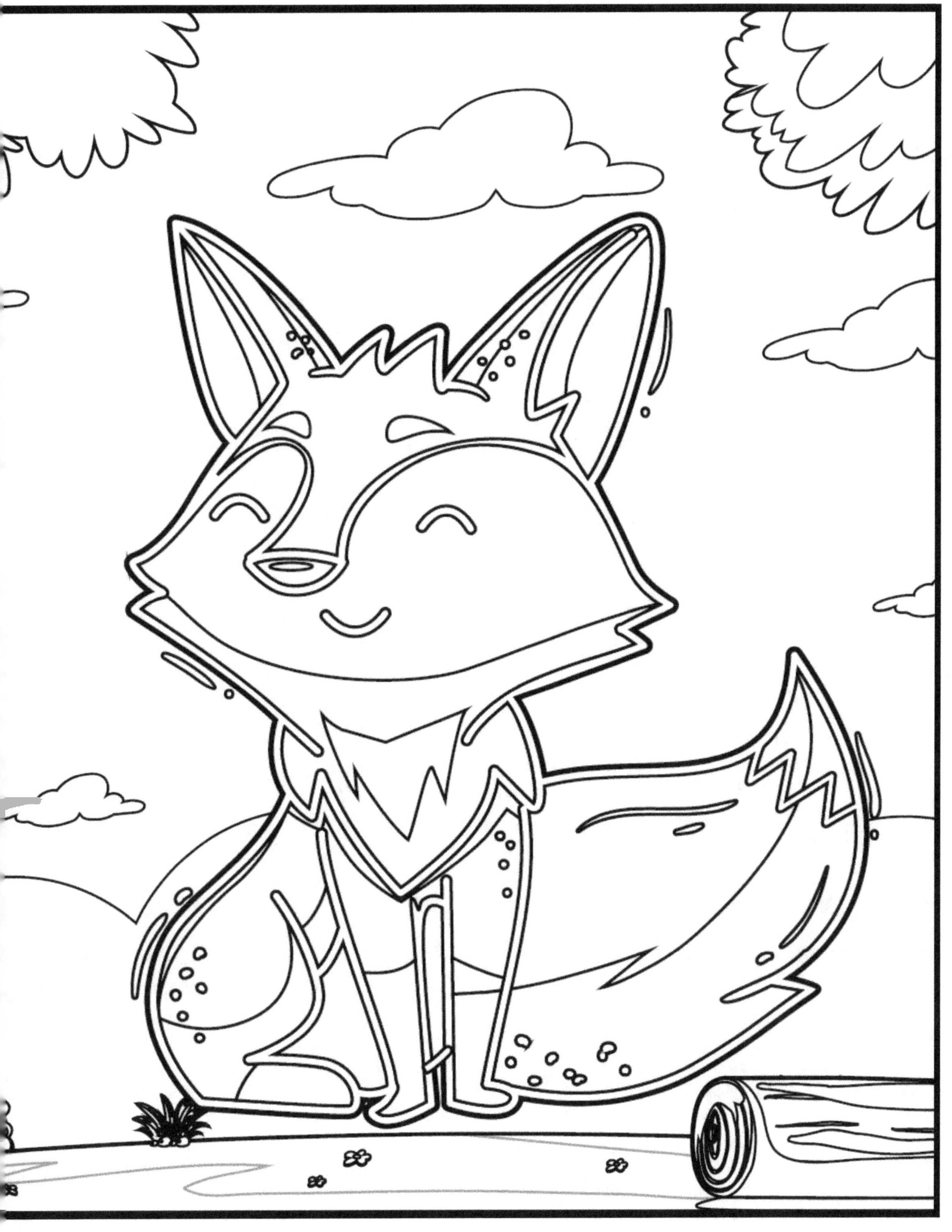

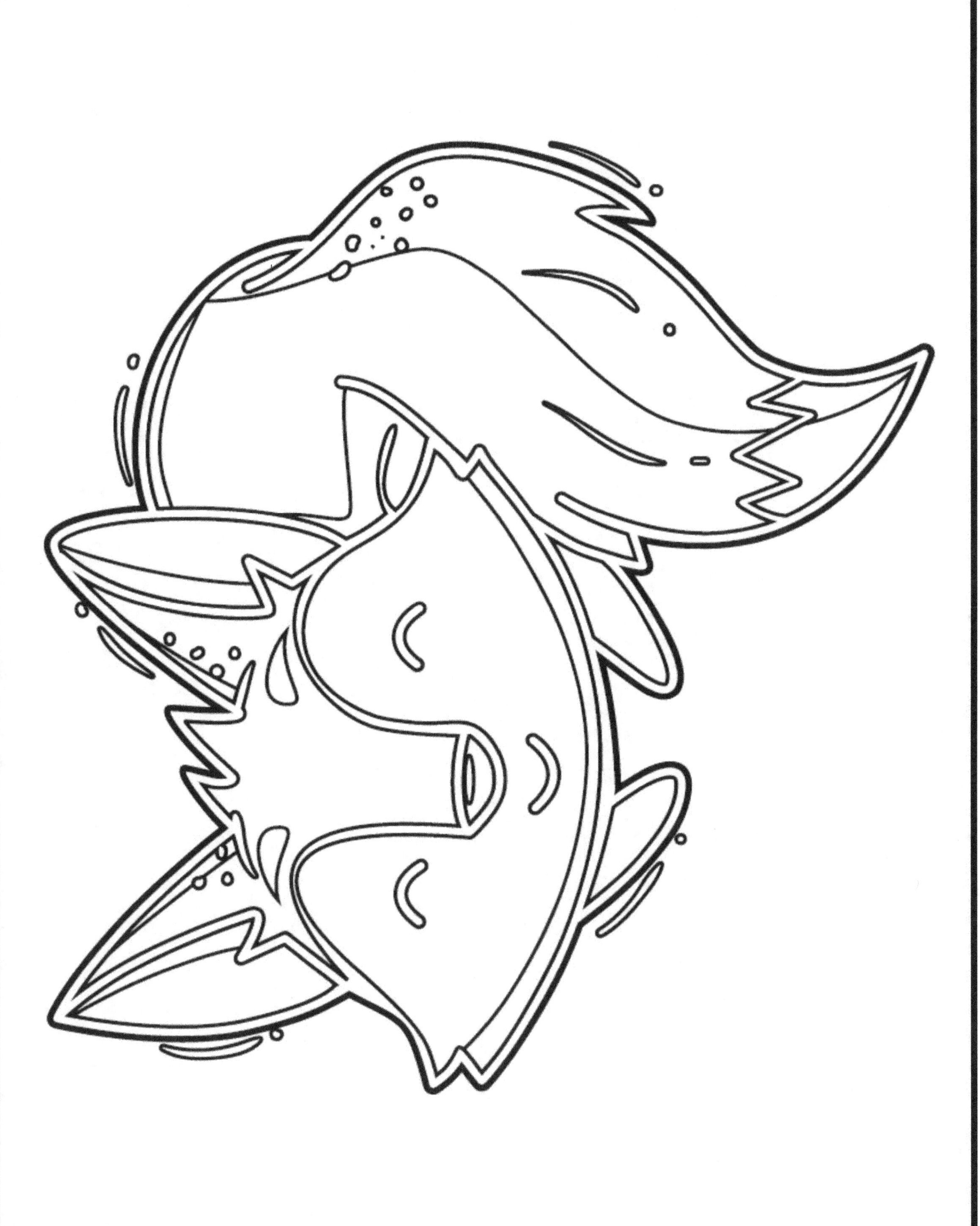

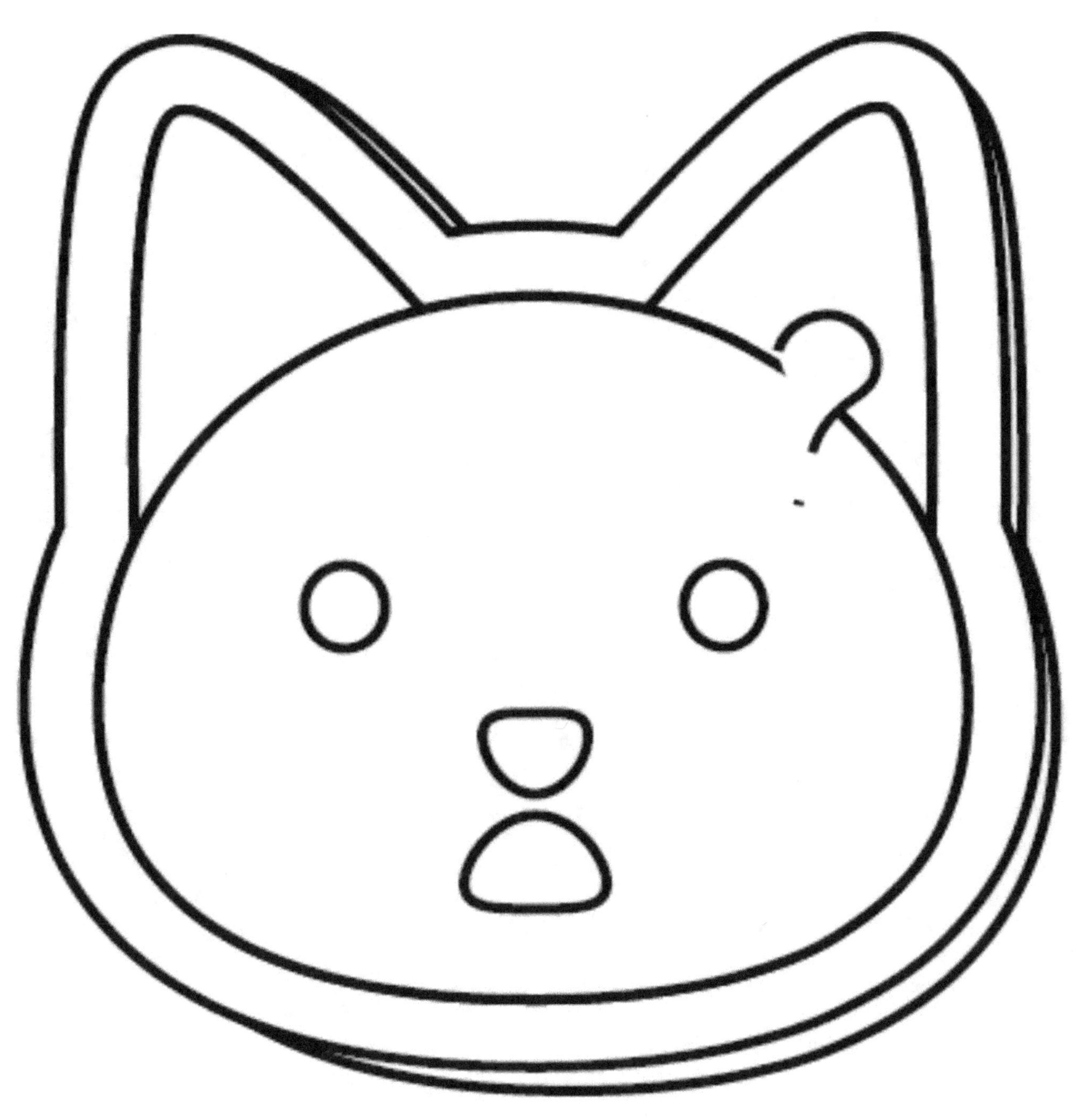

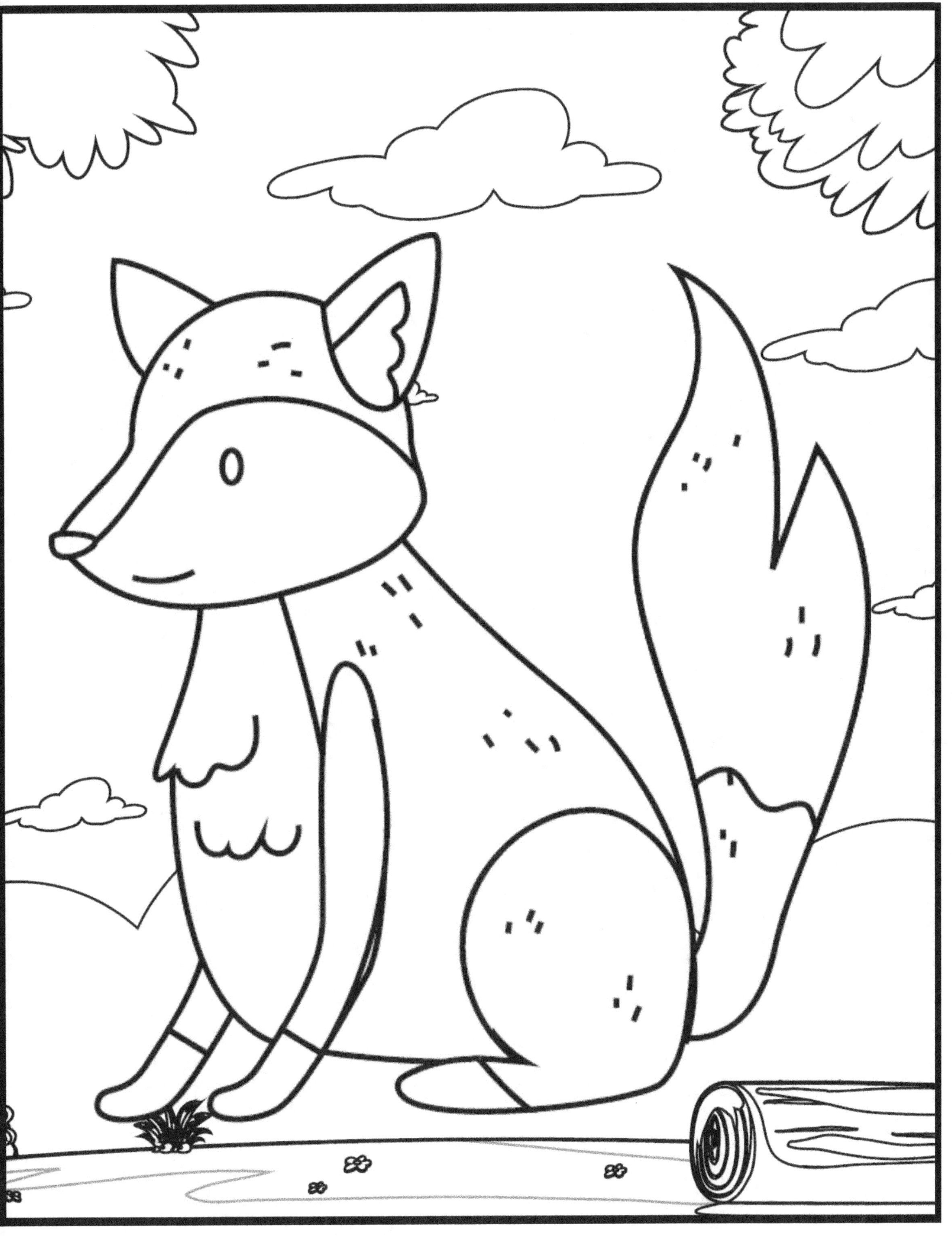

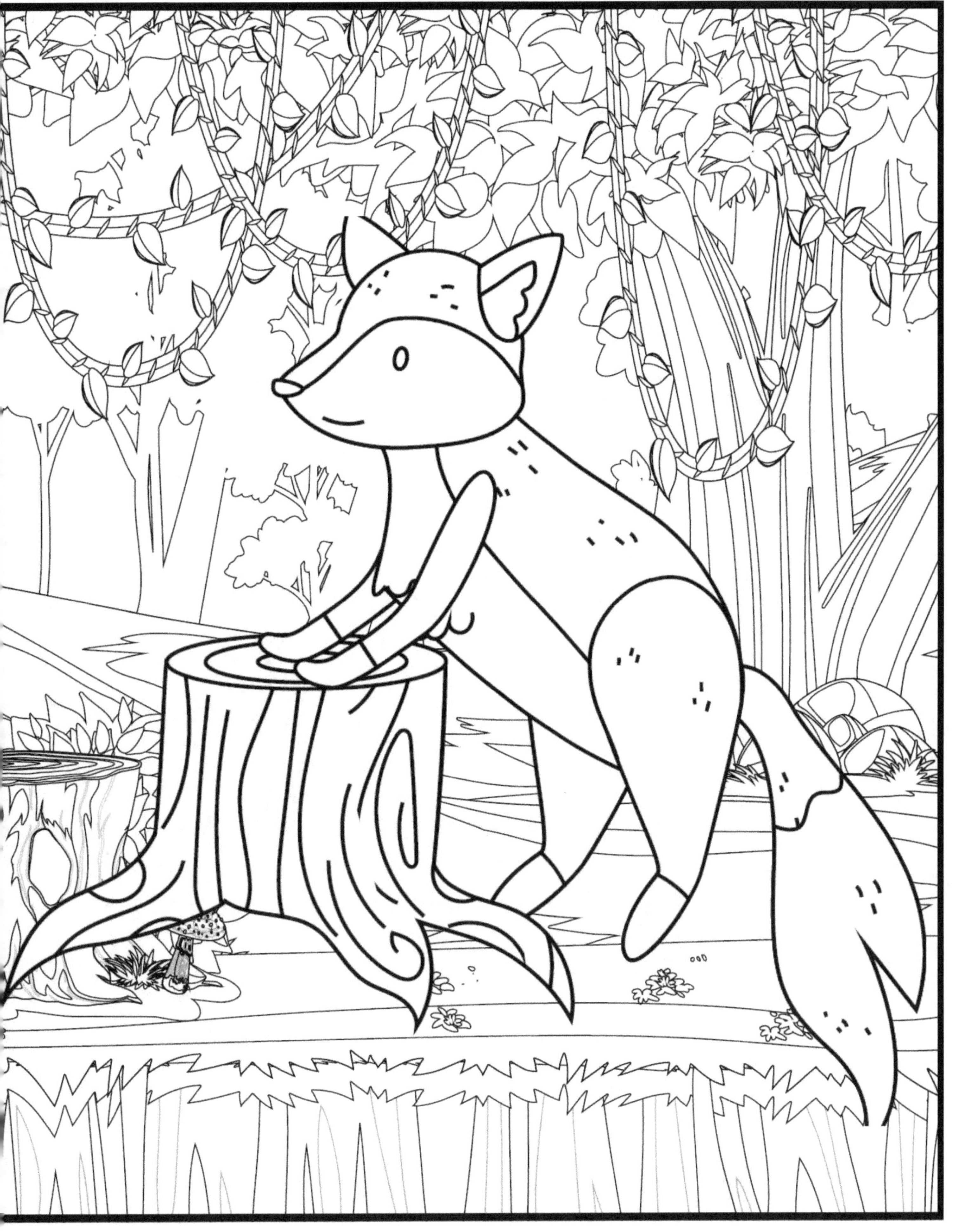

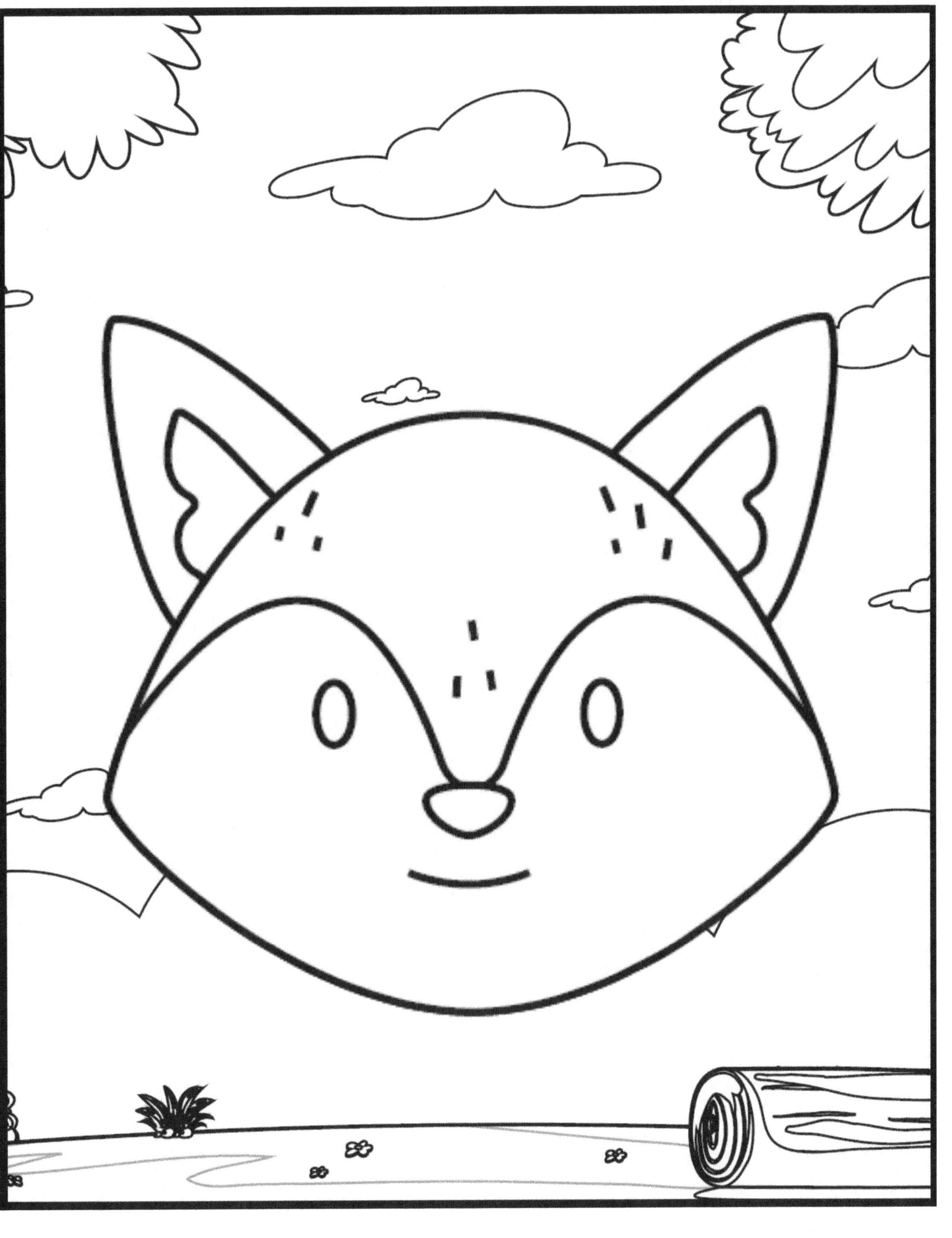

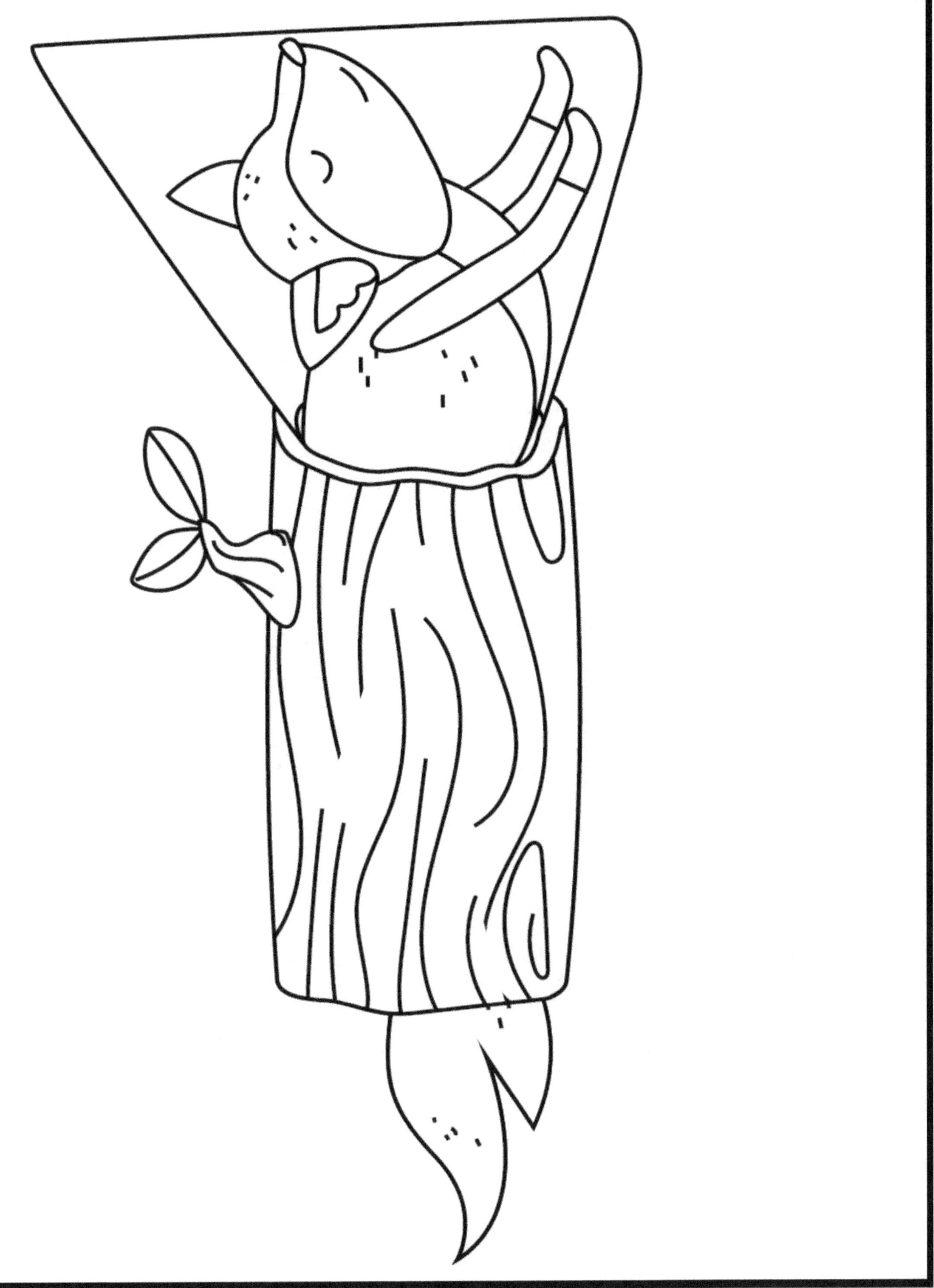

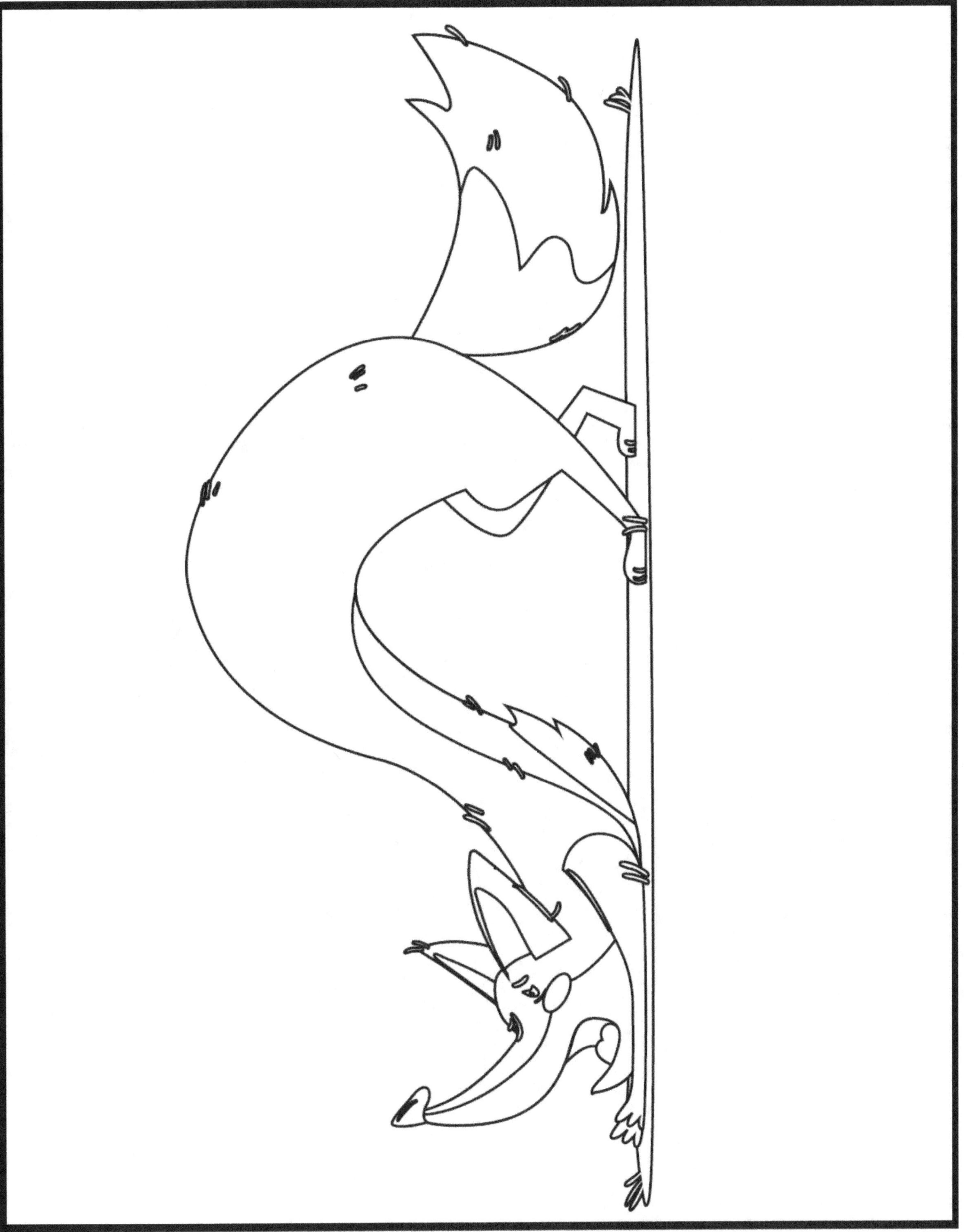

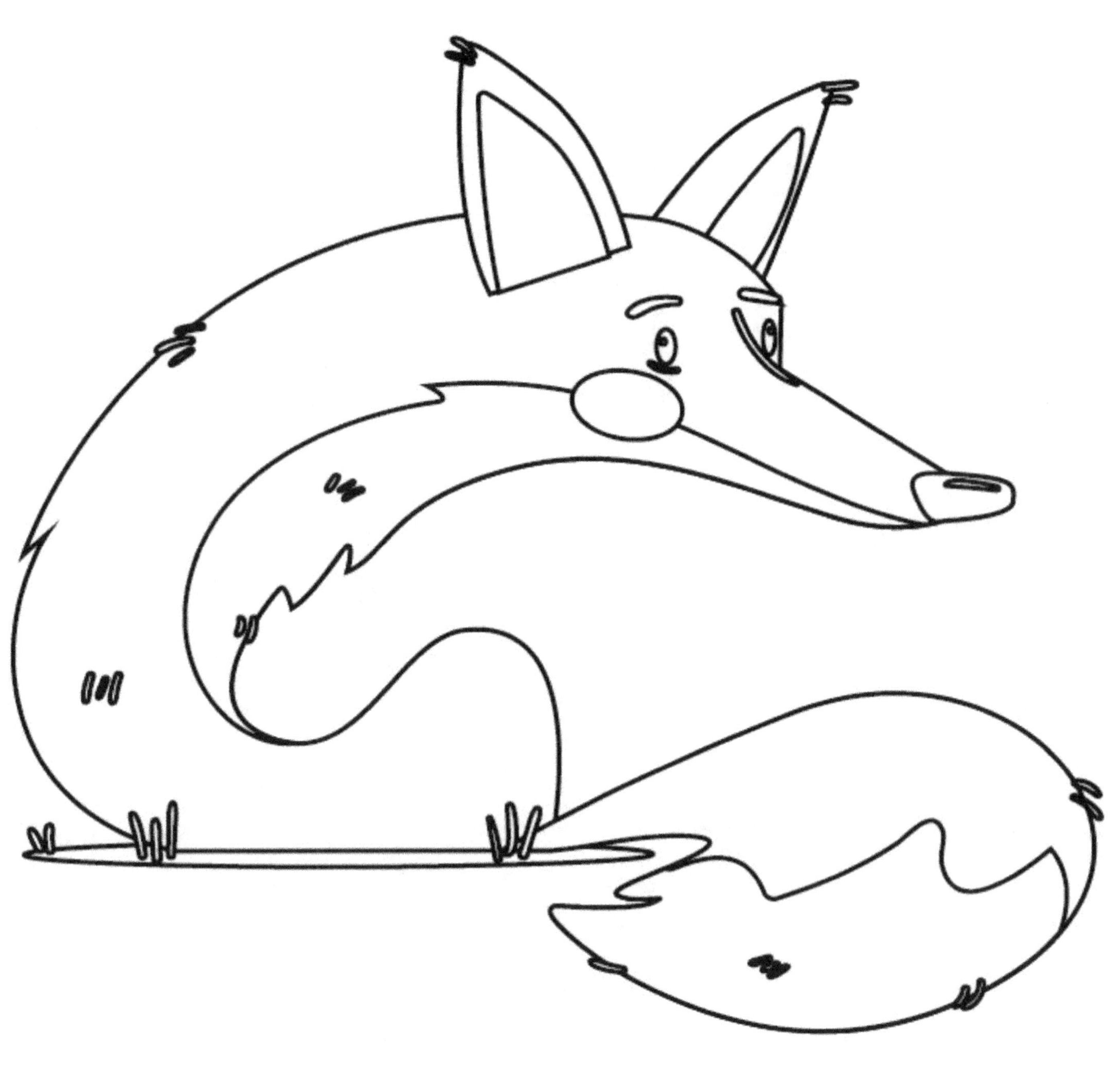

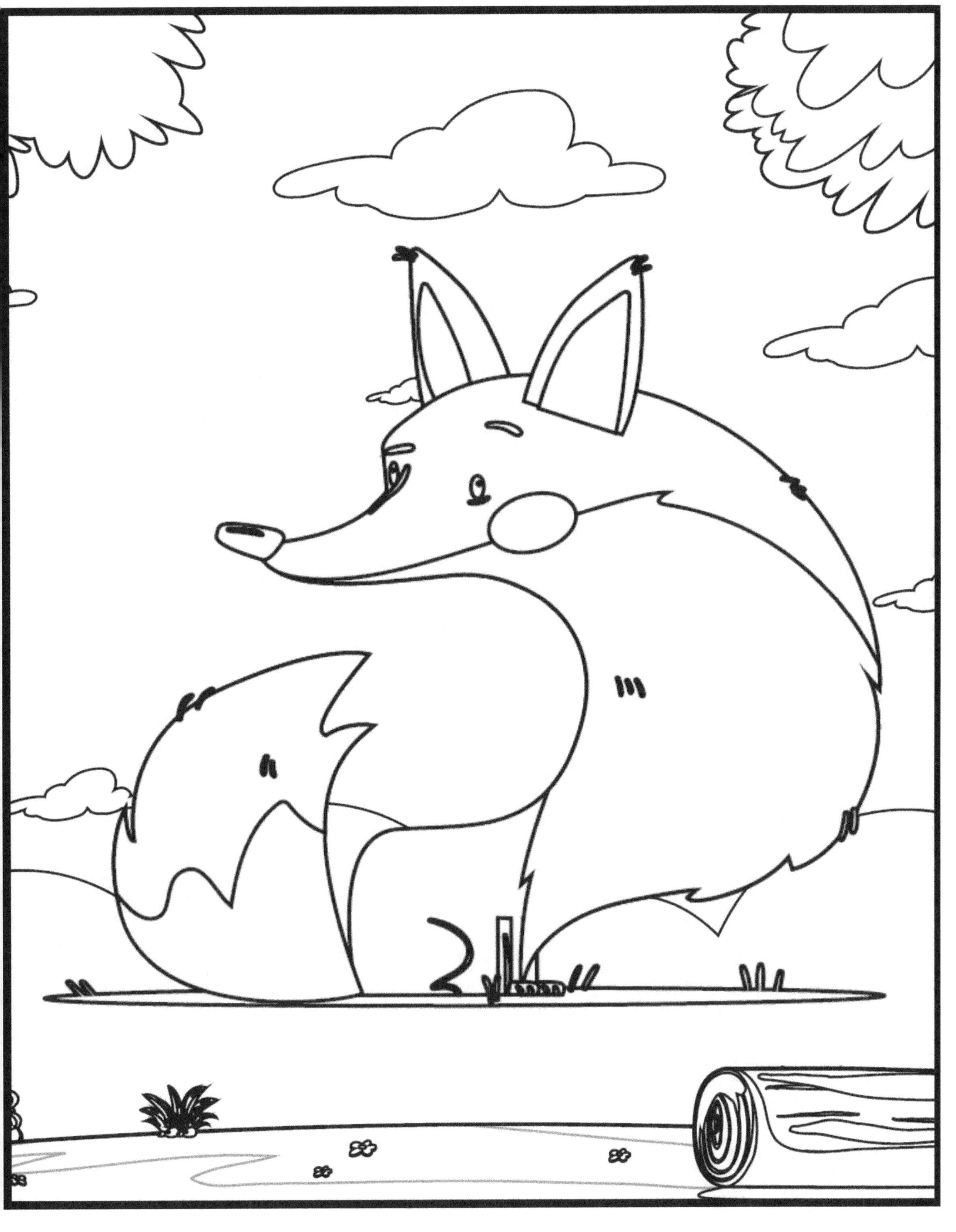

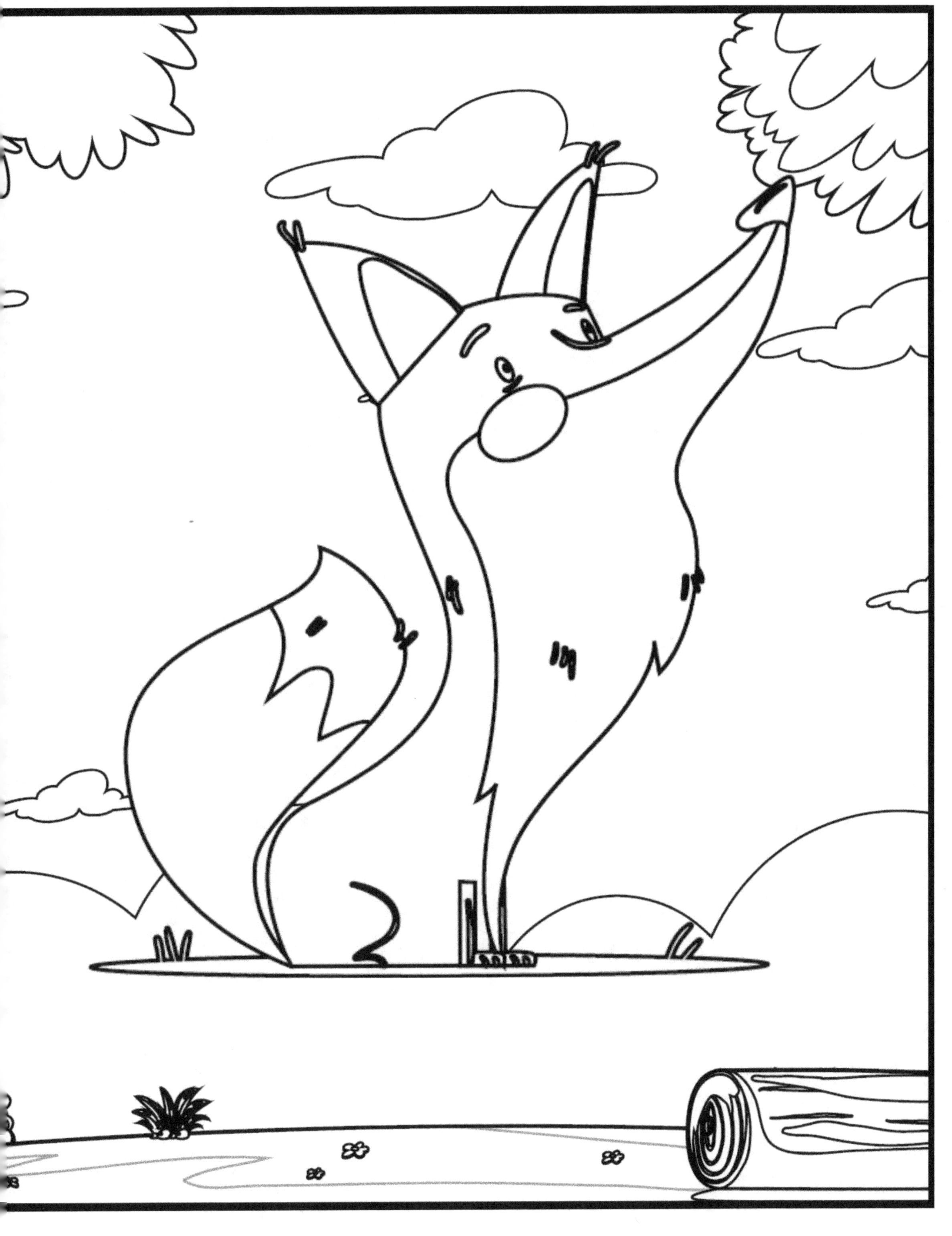

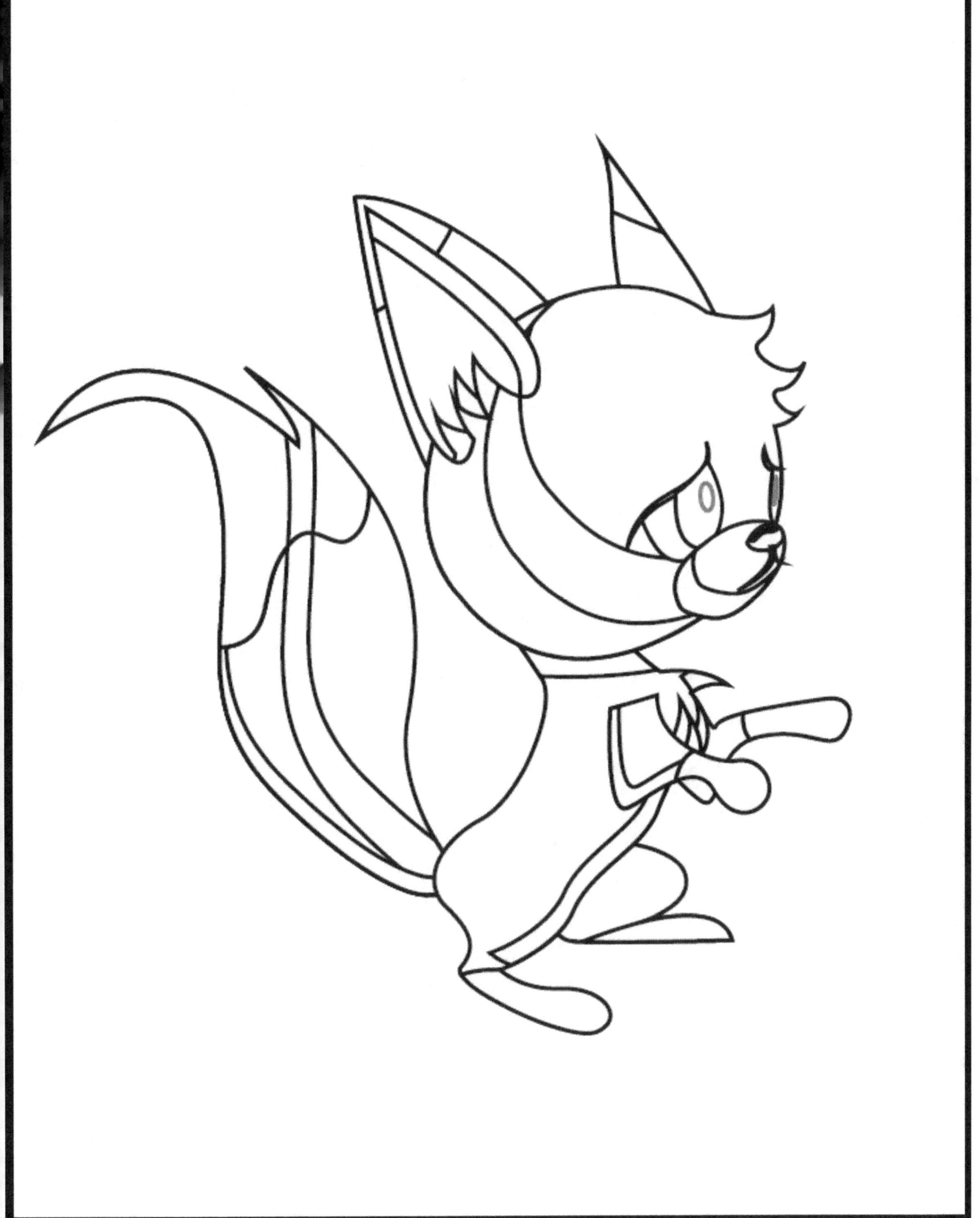

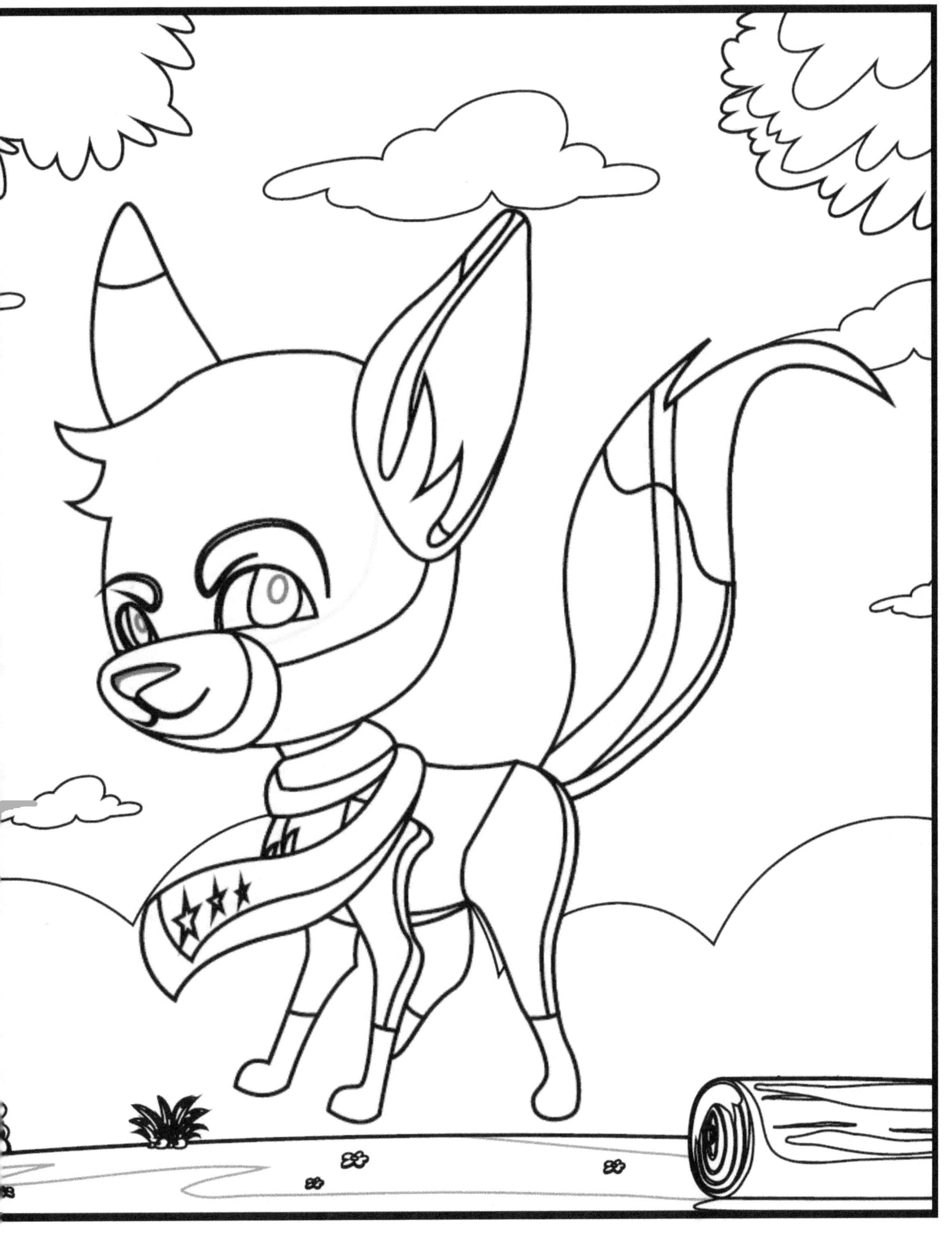

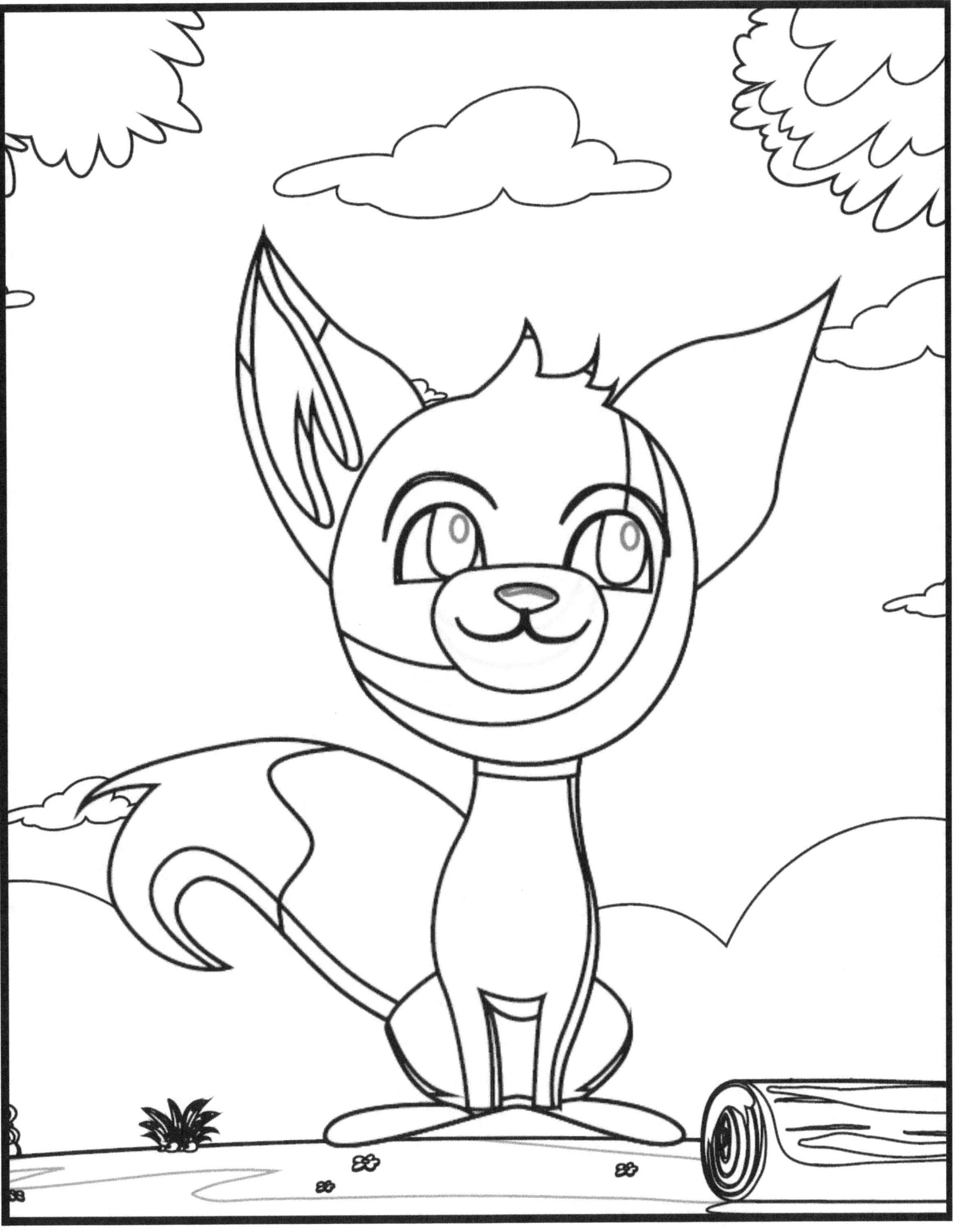

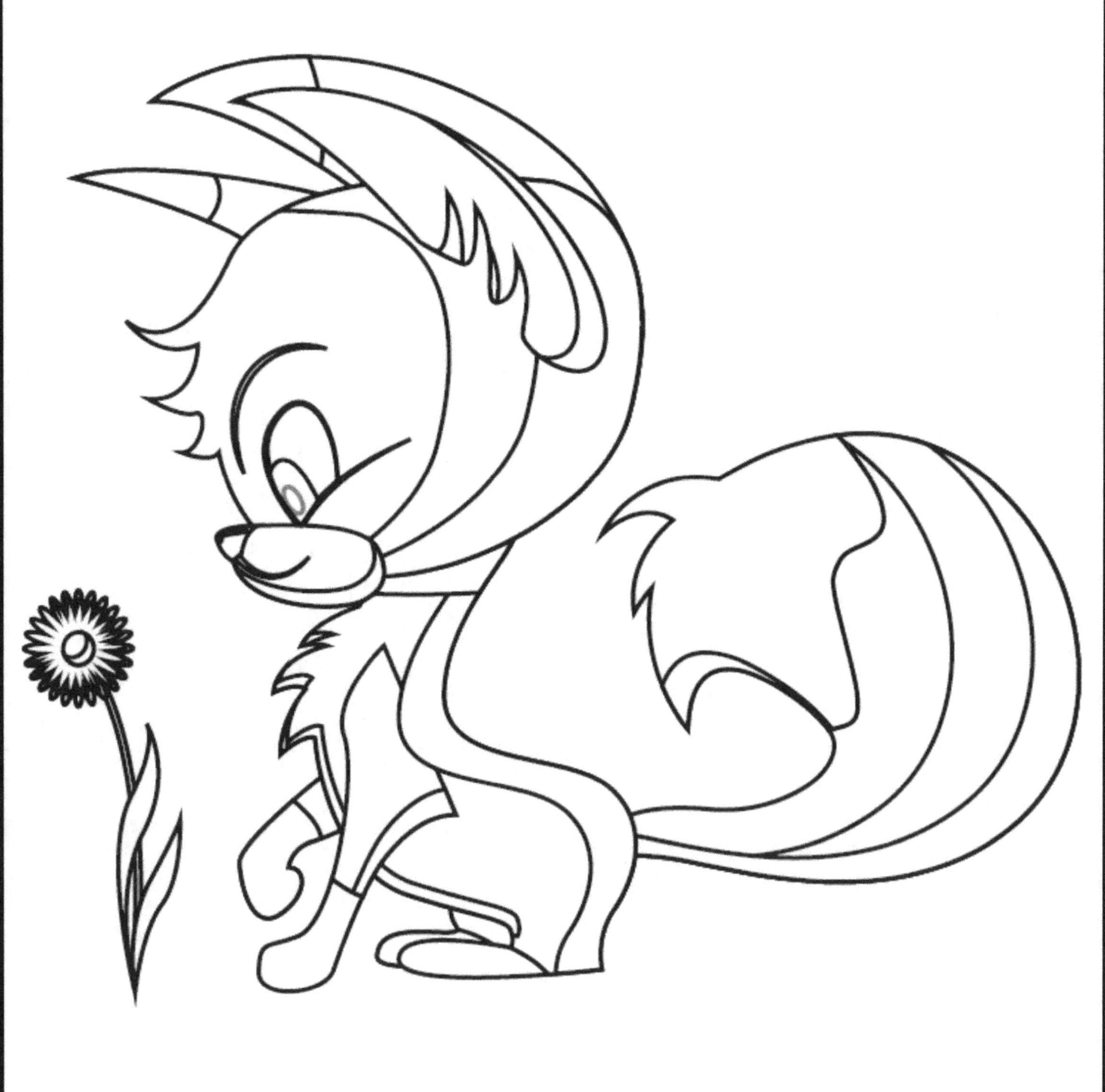

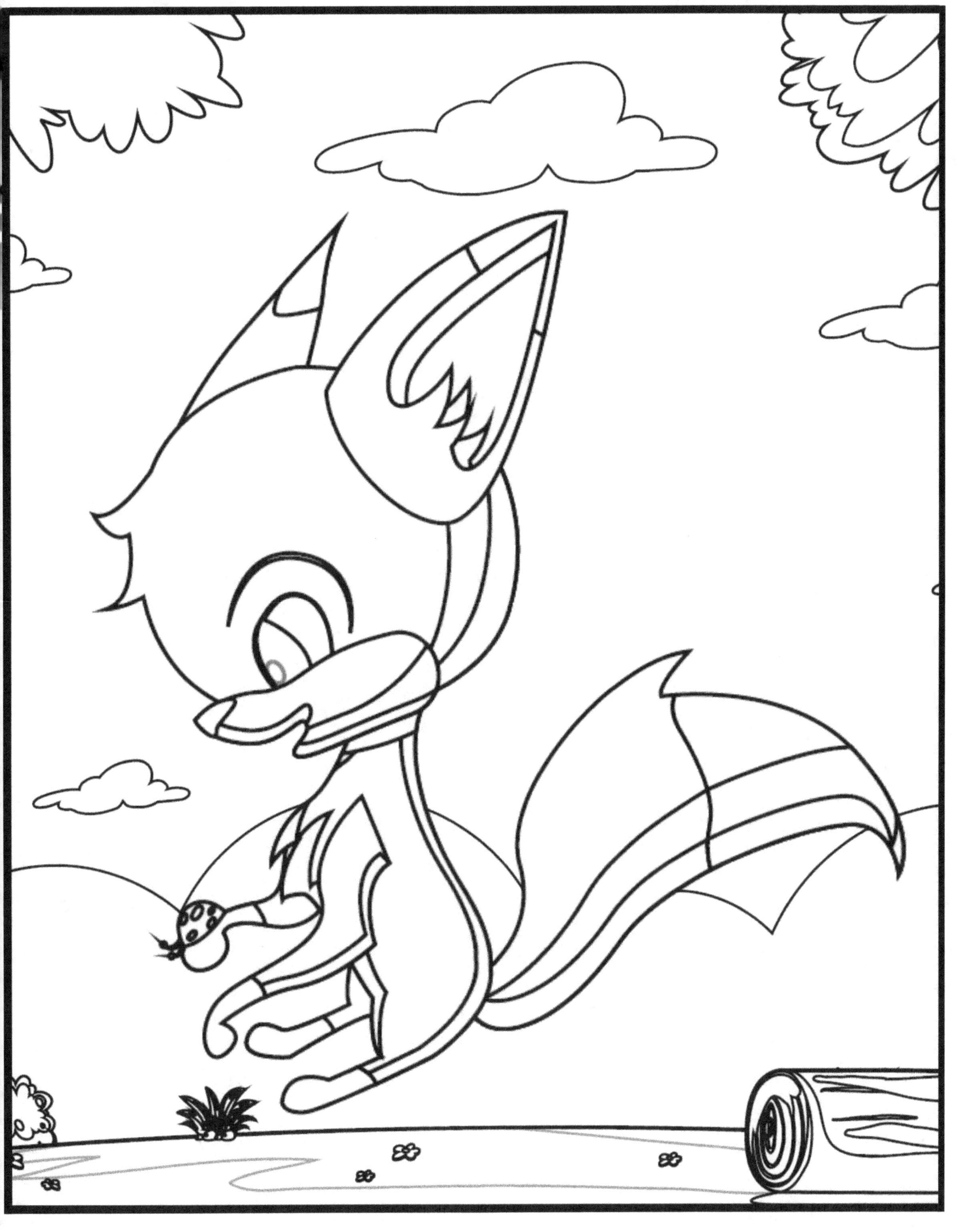

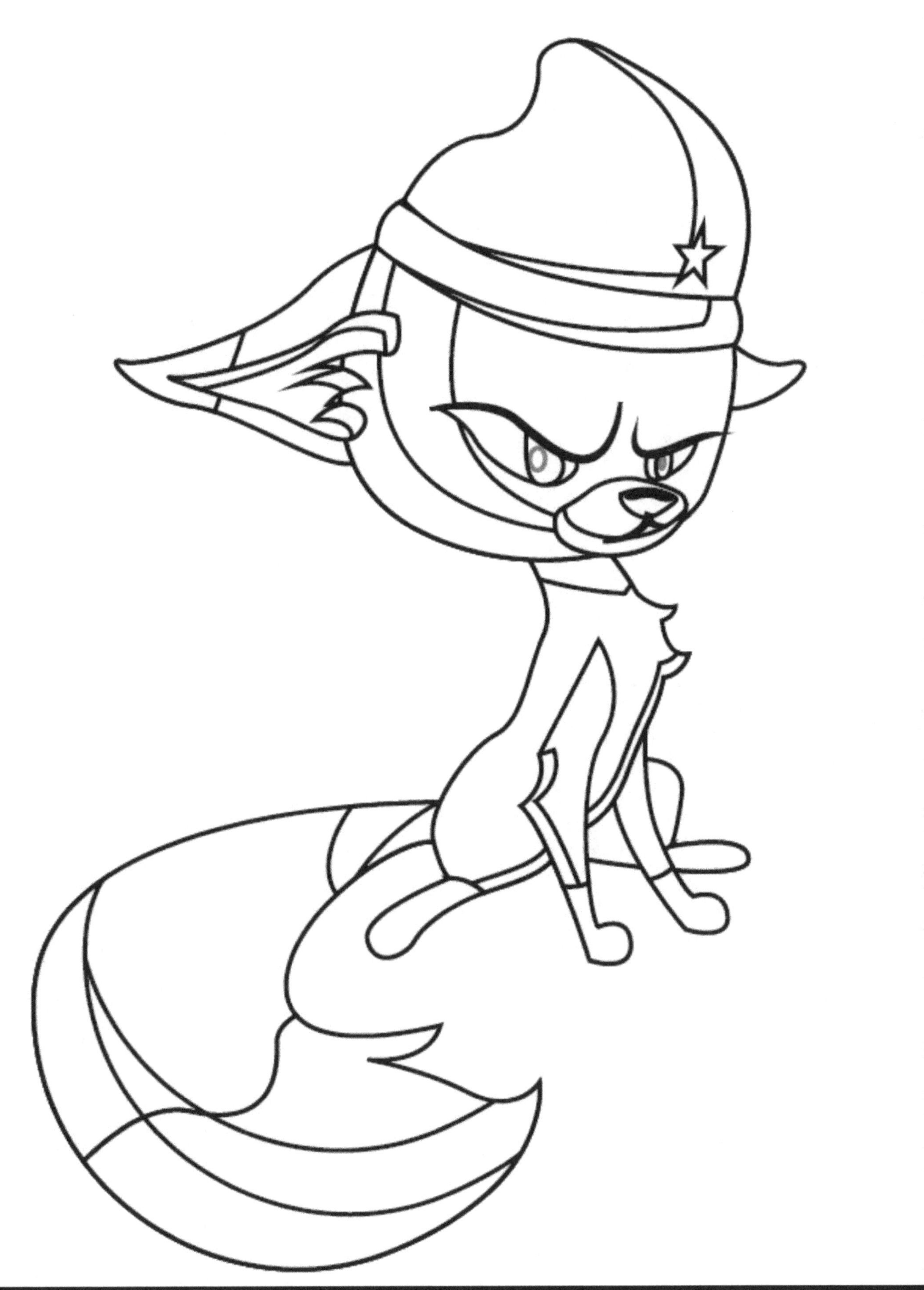

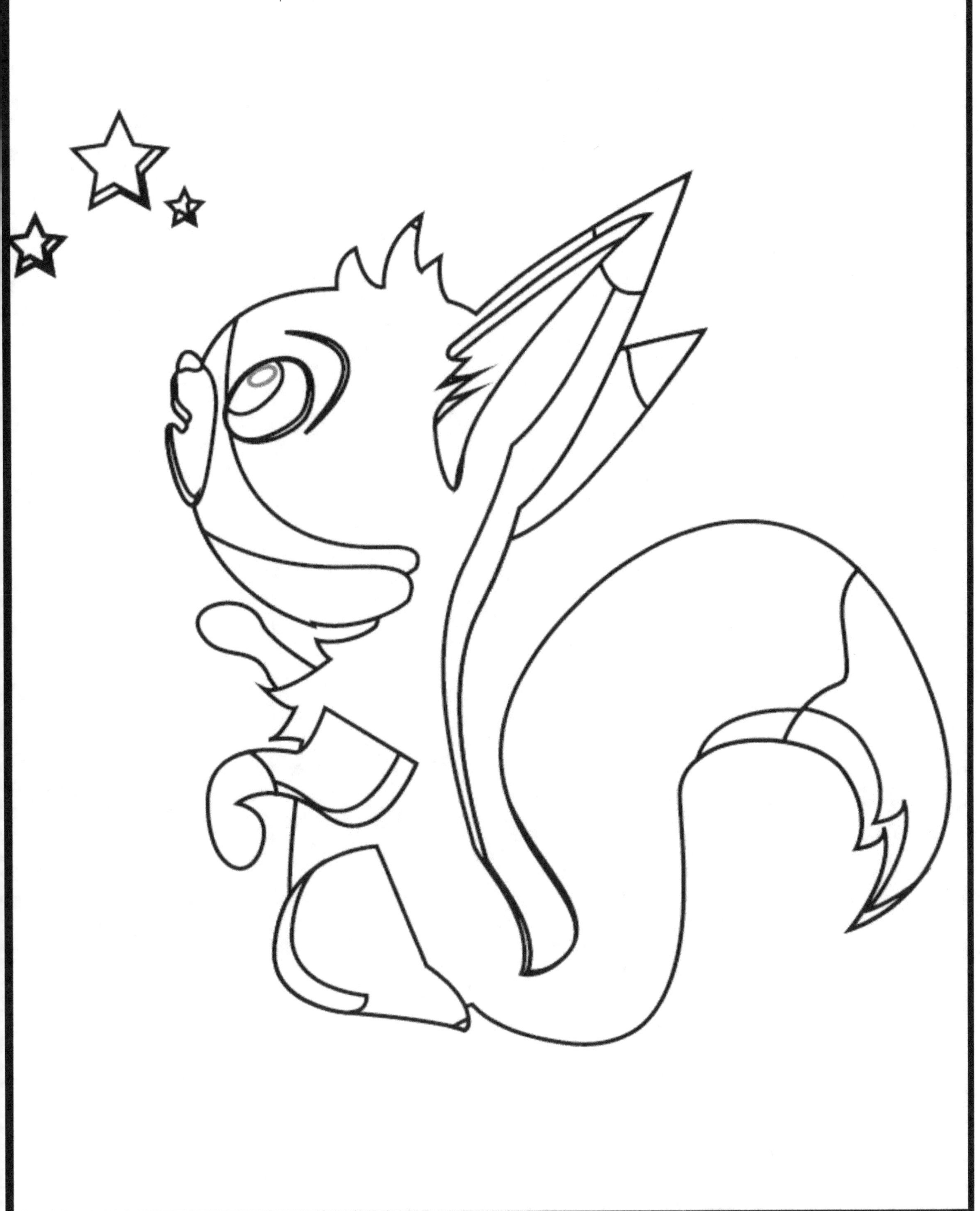

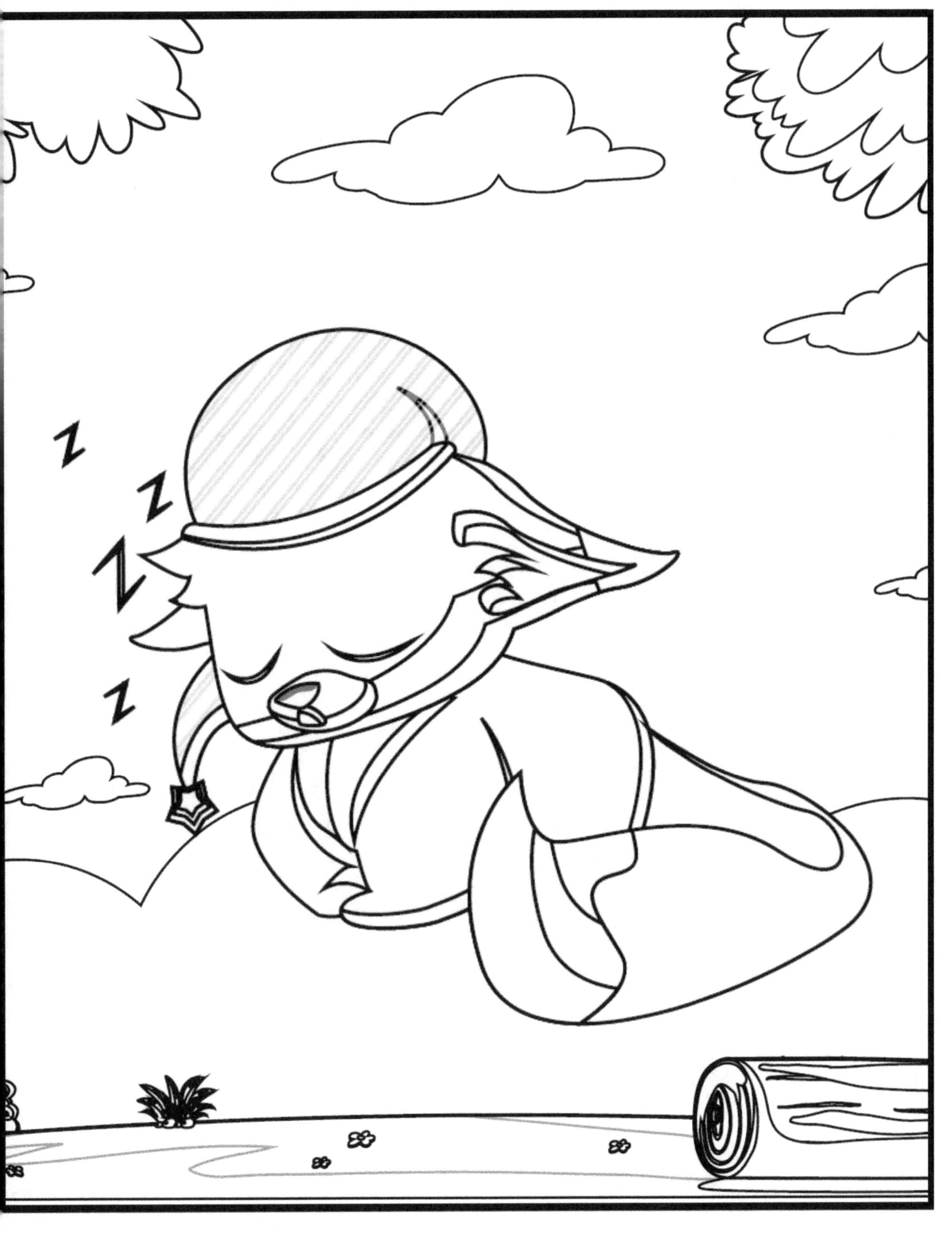

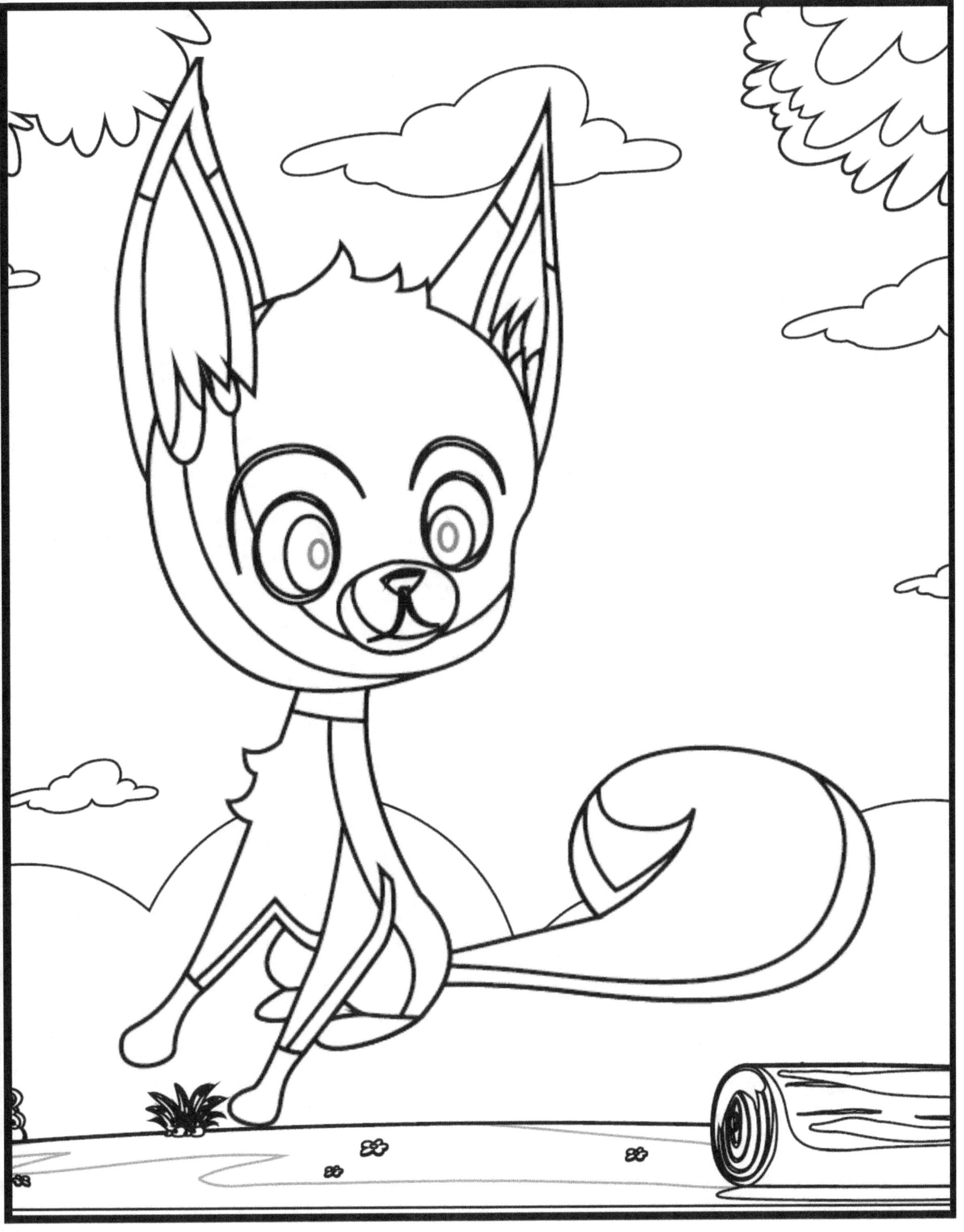

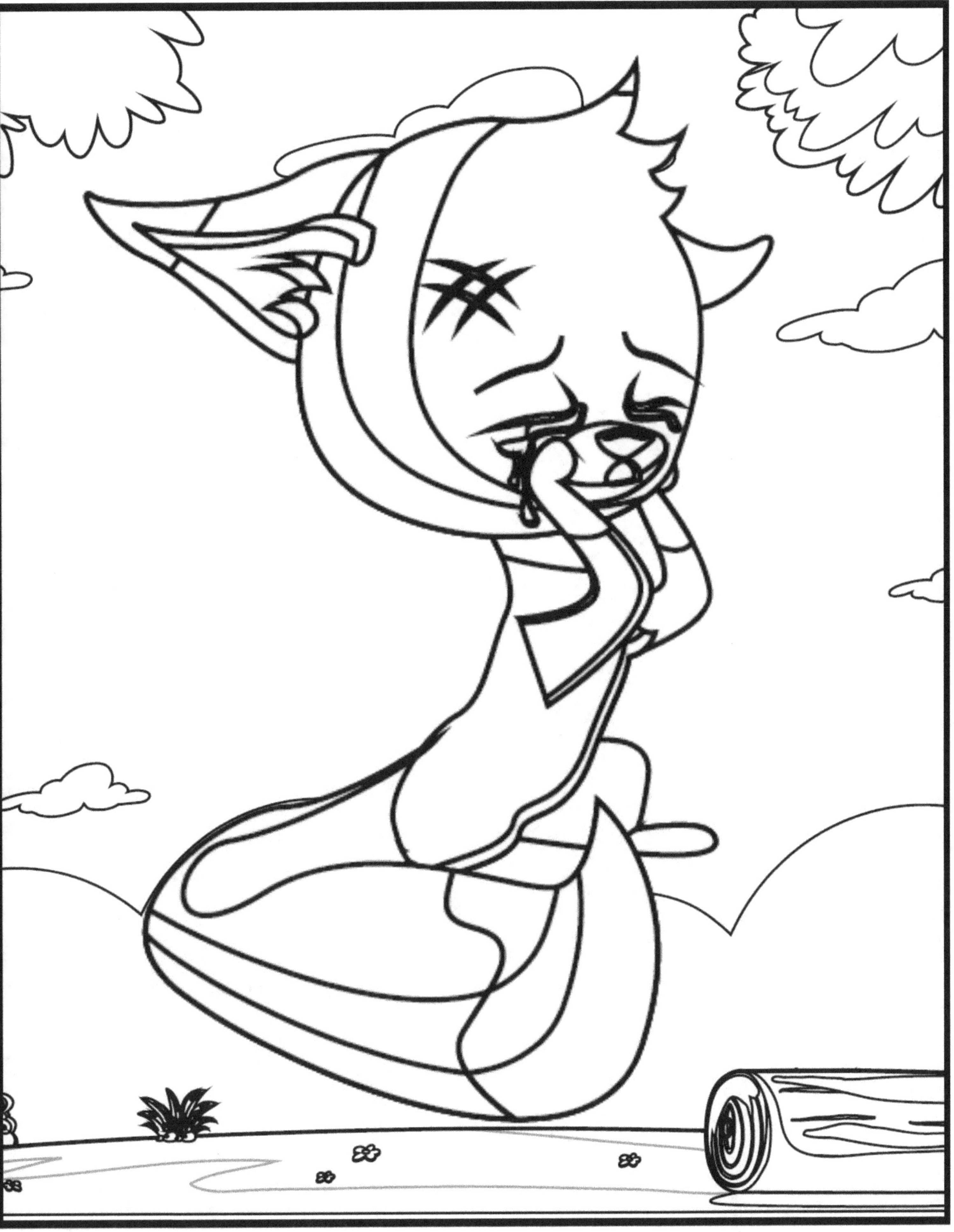

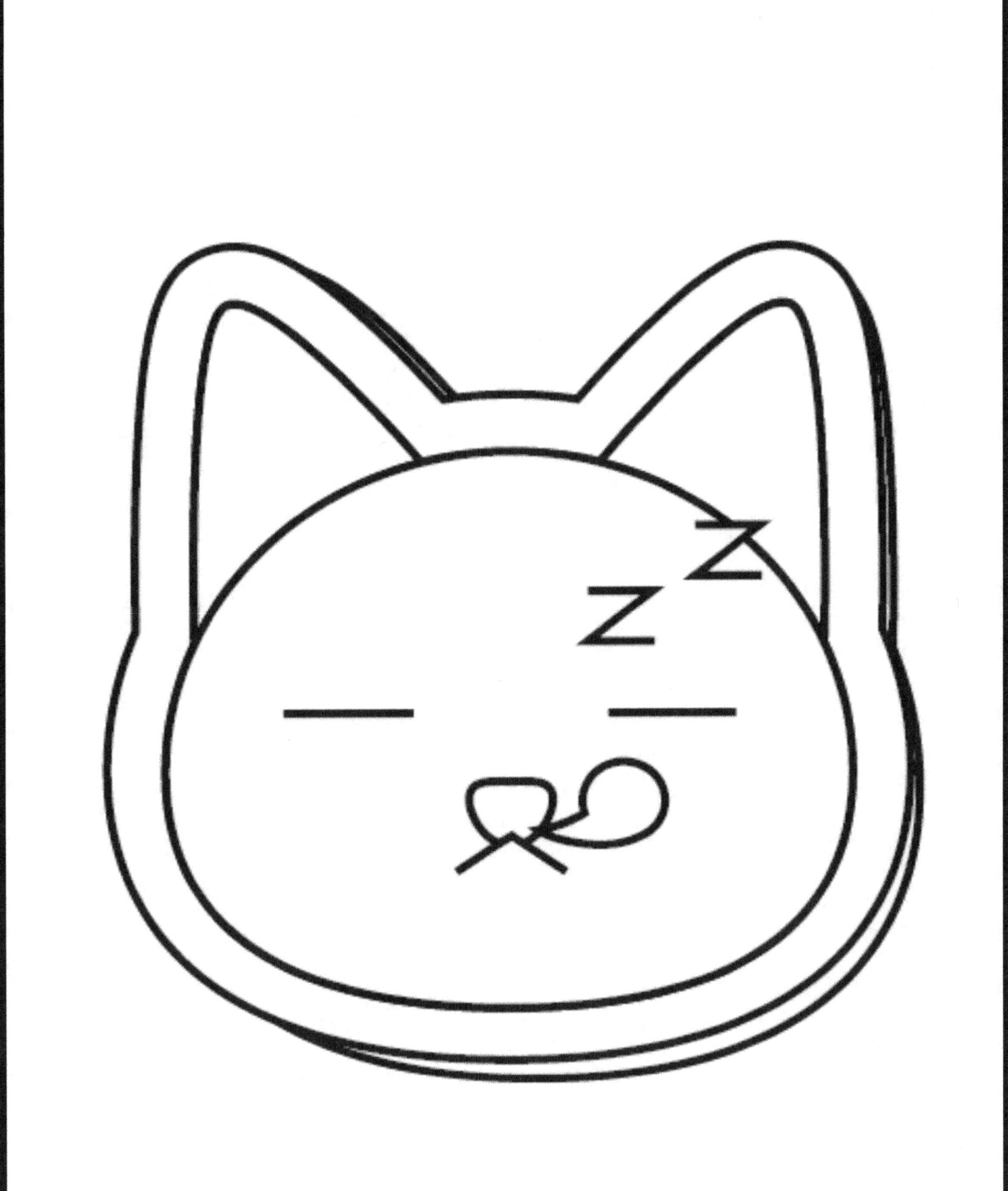

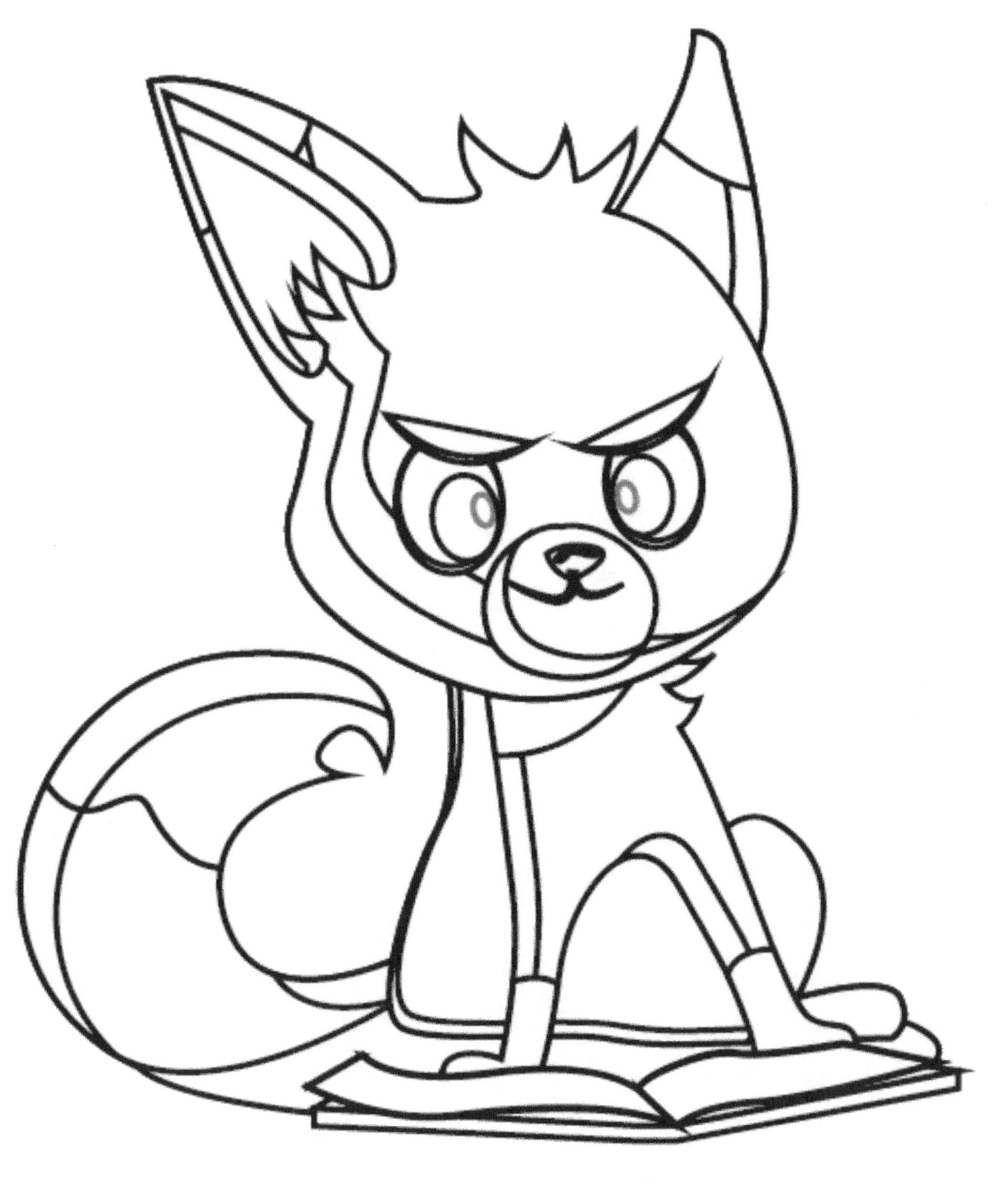

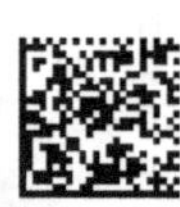

9798705840809